Advanced T'ai-Chi Form Instructions

Cheng Man-Ch'ing's Advanced T'ai-Chi Form Instructions

With Selected Writings
on Meditation,
the *I ching*, Medicine
and the Arts

*Compiled and translated
by Douglas Wile*

Copyright © 1985 by Douglas Wile
ISBN 0-912059-03-6

All rights reserved. No part of this book may be reproduced or transmitted in any form or by any means, electronic or mechanical, including photocopying, recording, or by any information storage and retrieval system, without the written permission of the publisher, except where permitted by law.

First edition, spring, 1985
Second edition, winter, 1986
Third edition, summer, 1986
15 14 13 12 11 10 9 8 7 6 5

Published by
Sweet Ch'i Press
662 Union St.
Brooklyn, New York 11215

Acknowledgements

Louis Alfalla, William Brown, Hung Ming-shui,
Liang Chin-huan, Louise Lippin, Lu Hung-pin,
Sara Rogers, Zack Rogow, Lena Valentino-Brandt

for Janet and Abraham

Other titles from Sweet Ch'i Press
of interest to readers of this book:

Master Cheng's Thirteen Chapters on T'ai-chi ch'üan
T'ai-chi Touchstones: Yang Family Secret Transmissions

Translator's Note

This is the third in our series of translations intended to bring seminal and significant works on T'ai-chi ch'üan to English-speaking practitioners. Here we return again to the legacy of Cheng Man-ch'ing, presenting previously untranslated portions of his *Thirteen Chapters (Cheng Tzu T'ai-chi ch'üan shih-san p'ien)*, additional material from his later *New Method of Self-Study for T'ai-chi ch'üan (Cheng Tzu T'ai-chi ch'üan tzu-hsiu hsin-fa)*, and relevant writings on meditation, medicine, the *I ching*, and the arts. The purpose of this present collection, then, is twofold: to present for the first time in English the form and self-defense instructions as they appear in his original Chinese manuals, and to introduce a wider spectrum of his thought and teachings.

Part One of this book, prefatory material from the *Thirteen Chapters* and *New Method*, reinforces and supplements many of the principles in the "thirteen chapters" themselves. Topics include: teaching techniques and learning attitudes, history and development of the Cheng form, clarification of such terms as *"ch'i"* and "internal," the role of acupoints and meridians, Chinese and Western medicine in relation to T'ai-chi, superiority of T'ai-chi over other systems, explication of the "T'ai-chi Classics," inner alchemy, supplementary exercises, and the participation of women in T'ai-chi.

Part Two, chapters XVI through XIX, represents the form and applications instructions from Cheng's original *Thirteen Chapters,* augmented by passages in brackets from his *New Method* where there are significant differences. Comparing form instructions in the *Thirteen Chapters* with later versions in Chinese or English, the former are richer in theoretical detail and present the applications as an integral aspect of the postures. The earliest work introducing Cheng's teacher, Yang Ch'eng-fu's form and teachings, *The Art of T'ai-chi ch'üan (T'ai-chi ch'üan shu),* published in 1925 by Ch'en Wei-ming, did not integrate application images in the form text. Yang sought to remedy this omission by bringing out his *Self-Defense Methods of T'ai-chi ch'üan (T'ai-chi ch'üan shih-yung fa,* preface dated 1933), devoted solely to Push-hands and a series of 37 self-defense applications. Yang's next work, *Complete Form and Applications of T'ai-chi ch'üan (T'ai-chi ch'üan t'i-yung ch'üan-shu,* published in 1934 and possibly ghost written by Cheng) consolidated the form and applications into a single narrative, creating, in effect, a two-person exercise consisting of one actual and one hypothetical partner. Thus lyric and melody were reunited; story-line and dance rejoined. Cheng's *Thirteen Chapters* closely follows this point/counter-point format, but goes more deeply into movement principles and *ch'i* circulation. Subsequent presentations of Cheng's form omit both self-defense visualizations and much of the advanced theory, concentrating instead on a more detailed display of gross mechanics. The *Thirteen Chapters* was concerned with rationalizing and preserving the subtleties of the art; later versions aimed for wide dissemination.

In addition to self-defense images, Cheng's original form instructions contain a number of principles not found as such in the "T'ai-chi Classics," and rarely heard today. Let us pry just one gem from its setting by way of example: the concept of "movement and swing" *(tung tang)* explained in his *New Method* under the instructions for Grasp Sparrow's Tail and "Important Points for Self-Study." This principle, if properly understood, can revolutionize one's execution and experience of the form. Impetus mobilized from center produces movement and momentum. Momentum, or intertia, is what Cheng calls "swing." Before each swing reaches its peak, a new impetus initiates the next movement, and for a transitional instant, the waning swing and waxing movement may actually be opposed. The new finally overwhelms the old, like the ebbing of a spent wave slipping back into the sea, even as the next breaker crashes over it. T'ai-chi ch'üan is not simply slow-motion or legato; principles like *tung tang* allow continuous connection with center, for gears to mesh and directions to change without passing through neutral, coming to a halt, or loss of power potential. We might also compare this movement quality to cracking a long whip. The handle sends the lash out in one direction, but to prevent its falling to the ground when the momentum is exhausted, it must be snapped back in the opposite direction before the popper reaches its peak. In T'ai-chi the snaps are internal and all but invisible.

Chapter XX is a translation of two articles by Cheng on meditation. According to traditional Chinese nomenclature, meditation belongs to the category of "sitting practices" *(ching-kung)*, as opposed to *tung-kung* or "moving practices," such as T'ai-chi ch'üan. Cheng came to sitting practice somewhat late in life, as evidenced by the following comment in the *Thirteen Chapters:* "If we compare it [T'ai-chi] to meditation, it does not have the negative effect of wearing out the *ch'i* for the sake of easing the body." In the articles which appeared in 1968, Cheng tells us that he was introduced to meditation and various works on inner cultivation *(nei-kung)* five years earlier. Thus he took up sitting meditation more than thirty years after his formative period in T'ai-chi ch'üan. Cheng was older and the times had changed. During the 30s and 40s when China was engaged in civil war and anti-Japanese resistance, Cheng spoke of T'ai-chi as a way of "strengthening the race and the nation," and of its "relevance to military strategy." by the late 60s, finding himself in a modern urban setting, he turned to meditation as a technique for "seizing a few moments of peace in the midst of this confused and stressful environment." His thrust is to demystify meditation, simplify it, and reconcile it with Western science.

Though already advanced in years, Cheng was still experimenting with new practices, still seeking self-improvement and ways to benefit humanity.

Part Three of this book is a miscellany of writings on subjects other than T'ai-chi ch'üan. Cheng's epithet, "the man of five excellences," was well deserved. Though best known in the West as an exponent of T'ai-chi ch'üan, articles in the Taiwan press usually referred to him as a painter and calligrapher who nevertheless excelled in poetry, medicine, and martial arts. In his later years he seems to have played the role of cultural ambassador at large. While it would be difficult to say that Cheng's impact on the world of letters and the visual arts changed the course of history—he was more interested in recalling tradition to its highest standard than breaking new ground—his influence on T'ai-chi continues to live and reverberate long after his passing. Cheng attempted to make his mark, too, in the realm of pure scholarship, the most esteemed of Confucian occupations, writing commentaries to the *Lao Tzu* and *I ching*. These likewise made little impression on the scholarly community, as they ignore modern methodology and concern themselves solely with the spirit rather than the letter of the Classics. His edition of the *I ching,* with commentary, shows his fervent desire to wrest the work from the hands of the metaphysicians and diviners and restore it to what he considered its original purpose: a practical guide for worldly affairs. Acknowledging the more than 800 major commentaries, Cheng singles out Ming scholar Lai Chih-te as the first in 2000 years to grasp the sage's true meaning, and Cheng bases his interpretation, especially of the "images," on Lai's.

Cheng in his early thirties was already an accomplished traditional physician, though not practicing professionally. Ch'en Wei-ming tells the anecdote in his preface to the *Thirteen Chapters* of Cheng curing Yang Ch'eng-fu's wife of a serious illness and thus winning the heart of the master. In 1939, temporarily "investing in loss," Cheng like countless other wartime refugees removed himself to the hinterlands, and being a man for all seasons, found his medical expertise most welcome in Chungking. Li Huan-sang in his preface to Cheng's *The Essence of Traditional Chinese Gynecology (Nü-k'e hsin-fa,* 1961) tells us that as a young man Cheng studied with a famous doctor, Sung Yu-an, and throughout his life consulted senior practitioners and perused old medical texts. In the afterword to his *Thirteen Chapters,* Cheng expressed grave reservations as to the desirability of woman participating in sports and public life, and recommends T'ai-chi ch'üan as the most appropriate exercise. This view reappears in his *Essence of Gynecology,* where in the preface he adds that the lives of women have changed so radically in the 20th century that old prescriptions are no longer efficacious. The chapter translated here, "Posterity," is an exposition of Cheng's views on sex and conception. This is Cheng's only published pronouncement on a subject of central importance to Chinese systems of health and self-cultivation. Cheng eschews both extrême Taoist teachings on sexual alchemy as a path to immortality and even moderate theories of the positive benefits of sexual yoga. Instead, he attempts to reconcile the traditional hunger for heirs with the negative effects of over-indulgence.

The selections from Cheng's *Three Treatises of Man-jan (Man-jan san-lun,* published in 1974) have been included in this collection for two reasons. First, these essays on painting and calligraphy make us realize that Cheng's accomplishments in T'ai-chi ch'üan were not accidental: he had been preoccupied with problems of eye-hand-mind coordination, with analyzing energy and its expression, and with the critical sifting of tradition even as a young boy copying out his characters. These excerpts provide a glimpse into the process by which Cheng was able to transfer insights and breakthroughs in one area of endeavor to his many other interests. In short, we are able to witness the mind at work which gave us the masterpiece of movement we know as the Cheng form. Second, students can continue that leapfrog process by creatively applying many of the principles discussed in relation to painting and calligraphy to their own practice of T'ai-chi ch'üan. The complex problem of reproducing a scene in painting is the same as the mimetic phase of form study. From his painstaking search for the true technique of holding the brush, we can better appreciate his emphasis on "beautiful lady's hand" and the thumb-middle finger sword grip. Whether the tip of the brush, the sword, or the finger, the mobilization and projection of *ch'i* is one. Can students of T'ai-chi ch'üan today hope to match his skill in T'ai-chi without equaling the subtlety of his mind?

In his approach to study and teaching, Cheng had something of a Confucian complex. The goal of a Confucian education was character development, promoted by means of the "Six Arts" (rites, music, archery, history, charioteering, learning, and mathematics) and the "Five Classics" *(Poetry, History, Rites, Music,* and the *I ching).* This curriculum was intended to produce the well-rounded gentleman of true cultivation. In peace time, the participation of this cultural elite in martial arts would normally decline, while in times of national peril voices would harken back to the necessity for training in "archery and charioteering." Cheng chafed under the stigma of ungentlemanlyness afflicting the martial arts and argued that T'ai-chi's embodiment of Taoist principles entitled it to a place in the temple of high culture. Cheng himself personified the ideal of the many-faceted gentleman, who pursued art not for art's sake, but for its usefulness or as a spiritual discipline.

Like Confucius, too, Cheng was not content to uncritically accept the inheritance of the past or to slavishly follow convention, but consciously set out to pan the stream of culture for its purest nuggets. He disapproved equally of those in former times who strayed from the true and contemporary compromisers. We may not go so far as to say that Cheng was a "prophet not honored in his own country:" after all, he was a senator in the nationalist government and a conspicuous if often controversial figure, but like Confucius he was cosmopolitan in his search for wider and more sympathetic audiences. Finally, like Confucius, he was a tireless teacher and transmitter, always looking for new techniques to communicate his learning and to discover the principles of learning itself. Indeed, we might well add teacher to his list of "excellences."

In his preface to *New Method of Self-Study,* Cheng borrowed a phrase from Chuang Tzu, "What I love is the *tao,* but I approach it through my art," and turning it around said, "Art approaches the *tao.*" The arts are whetstones for honing the *tao,* but without the *tao* there is no true art. For Cheng the painter and calligrapher, T'ai-chi was esthetic exercise; for Cheng the martial artist and physician, art was a study in the expression of energy. The pursuit of truth, beauty, health, and happiness was one. In this, Cheng was the quintessential embodiment of the Chinese ethos. It is hoped that this collection of his writings will not only nourish students in their practice of T'ai-chi ch'üan, but illustrate the rare convergence of a great culture and a great mind.

Prof. Douglas Wile
Brooklyn College
Brooklyn, New York
March, 1985

Contents

	Translator's Note	i
	PART ONE	
I.	Ch'en Wei-ming's Preface	1
II.	Teng K'o-yü's Preface	3
III.	Author's Preface	6
IV.	Forward	9
V.	Three Introductory Chapters	18
VI.	The Three Kinds of Fearlessness	23
VII.	Eliminating the Three Faults	26
VIII.	On What I Have Gained from Study	31
IX.	Dialogue with Disciples on Questions Concerning the "Treatise on T'ai-chi ch'üan"	34
X.	Questions and Answers Concerning the "Mental Elucidation of the Thirteen Postures"	38
XI.	Questions on the "Song of the Thirteen Postures"	41
XII.	Questions on the "Song of Push-Hands"	43
XIII.	Important Points for Self-Study	45
XIV.	Afterword to *Thirteen Chapters*	49
XV.	Afterword to *New Method of Self-Study*	53
	PART TWO	
XVI.	Advanced Form Instructions	55
XVII.	Push-Hands	101
XVIII.	*Ta-Lü*	107
XIX.	*San-Shou*	112
	PART THREE	
XX.	Selections on Meditation	114
XXI.	Selection on the *I ching*	126
XXII.	Selection on Medicine	130
XXIII.	Selections on the Arts	134

PART ONE

I. Ch'en Wei-ming's Preface

From
Thirteen Chapters
and *New Method*
of Self-Study

The famous painter, Cheng Man-ch'ing, is also a master of medicine. When Master Yang Ch'eng-fu came south he studied T'ai-chi ch'üan with him for six years. Once Madame Yang, nee Hou, became seriously ill and Cheng cured her with medicine. Master Yang was so thankful that he taught him all the secret oral transmissions. No one else had ever heard them. After arriving in Szechwan, he met an extraordinary man, studied with him and made great progress. One day he had a contest with fifteen American soldiers stationed in China. After defeating six of them, the rest were too frightened to continue. This became a celebrated incident at the time. After Japan's surrender, he came to the coast and showed me his manuscript containing Yang's teachings. Reading it I found the ideas excellent and most clearly set forth. Without departing from the original principles found in the "Treatise on T'ai-chi ch'üan," it showed students the path to follow. It accords with my *Questions and Answers on T'ai-chi ch'üan*. He was not secretive but made his knowledge public for all the world. Truly this is a precious raft for helping students of T'ai-chi ch'üan to pass over treacherous waters. Therefore I have written a few words for those who can appreciate this book.

Cyclical year *ting-hai* (1947),
4th month,
Ch'en Wei-ming

II. Teng K'o-yü's Preface

From
Thirteen Chapters
and *New Method
of Self-Study*

My friend, Cheng Man-ch'ing, is known as "the man of five excellences from Yung-chia." Although I have studied only martial arts with him, I was privileged to receive Master Yang Ch'eng-fu's secret transmission.

One day while in Chungking we both accepted the invitation of the British ambassador to give a demonstration of T'ai-chi ch'üan at the embassy. By coincidence, a visiting delegation of British soldiers was in attendance. They were all young strong military men and bold in spirit. Seeing that Man-ch'ing was short and slight, they underestimated him. I addressed them saying, "All of you gentlemen are large and powerful. Would you like to test yourselves against him?" They all agreed enthusiastically. The best fighter among them stepped forward to ask about the rules. Man-ch'ing answered, "Try anything you like." Thereupon he charged from several yards away, raising his left arm and waving his right fist. Man-ch'ing turned his body to the side, letting the force pass on the left, and threw him down several paces away. Again, raising his right arm and waving his left fist, he was thrown on the right side in the same manner. Finally, the man attacked in a very unusual attitude, aiming both fists at Man-ch'ing's head. At that moment, Man-ch'ing quickly tilted his head back, extended his right arm under the man's left armpit, and struck him. As a result, the man's two feet left the ground, and he fell backwards all the way to the edge of the contest area. Man-ch'ing swiftly caught up with him, and lifting him by the arm, prevented him from falling flat on his back out of bounds. Everyone was favorably impressed. The others stood by and did not dare to try him.

Man-ch'ing was asked to give another demonstration of his skill and he put out his right arm in the posture Ward-off. I announced that whoever was able to cause the slightest movement by pushing him would be the winner. One man pushed first but could not budge him. Another man joined the first, and pushing together for a long time, they still could not budge him an inch. He was then asked to give another demonstration. Man-ch'ing extended his arm with the palm facing up and declared that anyone who could grasp his hand and use pressure to prevent him from turning it over would be the winner. There were several volunteers, and with three attempts, three were thrown off by the turning of his hand. Then he extended his arm with the palm relaxed and invited anyone to hack at it with all their might. First, the strongest among them used a "standing palm" to attack it. After ten or so times he gave up, withdrew his hand and bowed out. Another gentleman raised his hand and chopped away several dozen times, but Man-ch'ing appeared completely unaffected. He was wearing a white ramie shirt, and the last gentleman, who happened to speak Chinese, rolled up Man-ch'ing's sleeve and asked if his arm was made of iron. Everyone applauded loudly and all marveled at the subtlety of our national martial arts, believing that they were matchless. This was the beginning of Britain's knowledge of the art of T'ai-chi ch'üan. Had not Cheng received the true transmission from Master Yang, would he have been able to perform such marvelous feats? His *Master Cheng's Thirteen Chapters on T'ai-chi ch'üan* is based on that true transmission. Moreover, he has discovered many things never before discussed. Just prior to publication he asked me to write a preface, so I relate this story by way of response.

Teng K'o-yü of Ching-shan

III. Author's Preface

From
*Master Cheng's
New Method
of Self-Study
for T'ai-chi ch'üan*

Others may speak of the way to good health, but few know the full significance. The chapter in *Chuang Tzu* entitled "On Cultivating Life" may be called the "Classic of Health." If we summarize his main ideas, they are the bed and the table. This is no different than Confucius saying that food and drink and man and woman are all there is. However, they did not really outline the principles. Only Ch'i Po said, "The true way is to eliminate old age and preserve the body. If one preserves the spirit within, how can illness find a way to us?" Describing the highest level, he said, "The muscles and pulse should be in harmony; the bones and marrow should be strong and solid, and the *ch'i* and blood obedient." He transmitted this to the Yellow Emperor who wrote the *Classic of Internal Medicine*. This is the "Classic of Health." Only T'ai-chi ch'üan demonstrates itself to truly correspond to the *Classic of In-*

ternal Medicine and the *I ching*. It correlates on all levels with the philosophical principles of Lao Tzu, the Yellow Emperor and Confucius. Moreover, it makes manifest the truth of both principles and practice. Were it not for the genius of the Immortal Chang San-feng, how could this have been achieved? There are foolish people in the world who would steal these treasures and claim them for this school or that sect. They are ignorant of the proper measure, for without true inner cultivation, how could one reach the level of "muscles and pulse being in harmony and the bones and marrow being strong and solid?" This is precisely what the "T'ai-chi Classics" call "collecting it in the bones until they achieve essential hardness and there is nothing they cannot smash." How can we expect those of ordinary intelligence to discuss this, or such concepts as "proceeding from interpreting energy to the stage of perfect clarity?"

I, Man-jan, was just barely alive when I began to study this art and was able to regain my health as if born again. It has been with me for forty years now without interruption. Moreover, I have gained a bit of knowledge of its theoretical principles as well. Every word rings true and there are no omissions. But alas, I am aware that the true Way has been little traveled for a long time. Some skeptics say that it has no practical function and cast it aside; some hold that it serves only health and do not look beyond this. They do not understand that the principles and applications of this martial art are as inseparable as form and shadow. If one studies, but cannot put his knowledge to practice, then what he has gained from the principles will be false. There is also a saying that in teaching others, one should hold something back, and that one may impart this knowledge to sons and not to daughters. All of this is pure selfishness. If we proceed in this way, our nation's culture and arts will gradually disappear or even become extinct. I refuse to believe this can happen. Have you not heard the words of the Yellow Emperor who said, "To find the right student and not to teach him is to lose the *tao*; to teach the wrong student is to waste the treasures of Heaven?" I hope that these words will reach those who seek to follow my way, that we may all be conscientious and encouraged.

IV.
Forward

From
*Master Cheng's
New Method
of Self-Study
for T'ai-chi ch'üan*

Some have asked me if it is really possible to master T'ai-chi ch'üan relying solely on a book and having no teacher. My answer is that this is a very good question. Self-study in T'ai-chi ch'üan is indeed very difficult. Former masters stressed oral transmission and personal instruction. But when there is no alternative, and in order to benefit the greatest number, one must not shrink from difficulties, but seek every possible means. Letters arrive like flakes of driven snow from students who are far away but seek the art of good health. It pains me greatly that I cannot personally answer each one, but in the midst of countless demands I have taken the time to prepare this book in order to fulfull my sincere desire. If one is only concerned with health, then this has already been addressed and does not constitute a problem. However, when it comes to self-defense, there are great differences as to depth and skill, quality and sensitivity. You may have to wait for another time, see how you progress, and seek opportunities for further improvement.

I remember many years ago I saw an old friend who has since passed away. His surname was Lin, his given name Pin and his style Fo-hsing. In 1936 we were both staying in Nanking, and at the time he was just recovering from an illness and begged me to instruct him in T'ai-chi ch'üan. I selected five postures—Ward-off, Roll-back, Press, Push, and Single Whip—and taught them to him. Shortly thereafter we were separated. In the summer of 1939 I arrived in Chungking, Szechwan Province, and Fo-hsing came to visit me. He demonstrated the whole form and asked me for corrections. I asked him where he learned this, and smiling, he answered that he had learned it from me. I replied that I had only taught him a few postures and the more than one hundred and twenty he just demonstrated were not learned from me. Fo-hsing said that after we parted he had obtained a copy of Master Yang Ch'eng-fu's *Complete Principles and Applications of T'ai-chi ch'üan* and continued to study by himself. I was very amazed. The results would be difficult to distinguish from those you could expect if I had personally instructed him myself. Moreover, the explanations for the postures and sparring methods were very complicated, and to have acquired them through self-study truly deserves our admiration. If we compare Yang's book to my *New Method of Self-Study*, then it must be admitted that mine is vastly simpler. If one practices carefully, there should be no doubt of success.

Based on my forty years of experience and careful analysis, I feel the ancients saying that, "The most important words are not complicated," is extremely profound. I remember when I was first studying T'ai-chi ch'üan, every day Master Yang instructed me saying, "Relax, Relax!" Or sometimes he would say, "You are not relaxed; you are not relaxed!" Occasionally he would warn me saying, "Not being relaxed is asking for a beating." Emphasizing his point most strongly he would say, "You must be completely relaxed." He could not have repeated this fewer then several thousand times. Within two years I heard these words so often that my head felt as big as a crock, and I hated myself for my stupidity.

One night I had a dream that my two arms were broken. I awoke in a state of alarm and tried them out. As if by a miracle I had realized total relaxation. The sinews of my arms were like a Raggedy Ann doll, and the joints seemed as if connected by an elastic band which allowed them to turn in any direction at will. Now if I had not felt that my arms were broken, how would I have come to know this state of relaxation? The next day I tested myself against far superior students, and they looked at each other in amazement. They inquired over and over and finally realized that I was indeed relaxed. I felt that in one day I had progressed a thousand miles. Thinking back on it today, Master Yang had great hopes for me as well as deep affection. Thus I know that the most important words are not complicated. But to truly grasp them is not simple. Without sincere faith and conscientious effort, even if one grasps them, they may not come to fruition. Therefore, although I obtained the marvelous results of this one word—relax—some thirty years ago, and fully explained it in my book, *Master Cheng's Thirteen Chapters on T'ai-chi ch'üan*, people still do not consider this a real secret, and to this day, those who have gotten it are very few. So I stress it again here and hope that those who share my aspirations will pay heed.

T'ai-chi ch'üan was originally developed to eliminate sickness and promote longevity. If its methods are good, then no matter who created it, it is good. If they are not good, then even if it were the work of the Yellow Emperor and Lao Tzu themselves, what is it to me? Some people have indulged in wild slander, claiming that T'ai-chi ch'üan was not created by the Immortal Chang San-feng 張 三 丰. I do not know what their motives are. At that time, T'ai-chi ch'üan was unique among the martial arts. Military training consisted largely of bare-handed fighting arts which were all transmitted orally through secret formulas or secret manuals, even to the point of teaching them only to sons and not to daughters. How is it possible to investigate these things and discover evidence or records? It is simply ridiculous. Furthermore, one of San-feng's styles was Chang Ch'i-chen 張七針 . We cannot use the names San-feng 三峯 or San-feng 三豐 , as these actually represent other people. I have very carefully studied the "Treatise on T'ai-chi ch'üan" and it is a perfect piece, inspired and natural. I do not know who else could have attained this state. (Thus the original commentary says that this is the treatise handed down by Master Chang San-feng 張三丰 .) He says, "If we want to raise something, we must first apply breaking power and its root will automatically break. Then there is no doubt that it will be quickly repelled." Without a profound grasp of Lao Tzu's idea that, "If we want to take something, we must first give something," how could he have reached such a penetrating understanding? From this alone we can see that there has never been in all the martial arts from the beginning of time such a marvelous application of philosophy to practical affairs. Who but San-feng could have attained this? This is what Lao Tzu meant when he said, "When the inferior man hears about the *tao*, he laughs. If it does not make him laugh, it is not the true *tao*." You can see my point. For this reason generations have honored San-feng as the first Master of Wutang.

T'ai-chi ch'üan is called the "internal" system. Bodhidharma is the father of Shaolin and his art is called the "external" system. This distinction of internal and external has been the subject of considerable debate for generations. Most of these theories are completely unfounded. They forget that the Yellow Emperor was the father of our race. Lao Tzu followed in his footsteps, and so we speak of Huang Lao [the Yellow Emperor and Lao Tzu]. San-feng took the philosophical principles of the Yellow Emperor and Lao Tzu and applied them to the martial arts. Therefore we call it the internal system. The Buddha was from India, that is, from a foreign country.

Bodhidharma was a Buddhist and therefore his art is called external.

T'ai-chi ch'üan emphasizes sinking the *ch'i* to the *tan-t'ien*. This is based on Lao Tzu's, "Concentrate your *ch'i* and develop softness. Can you be like a child?" The *ch'i* moves in the opposite direction from the breath, rising up the *Tu* meridian in the back. It first passes through the *wei-lü, yü-chen* and *ni-wan* points. This is the method based on "the inverted movement of the waterwheel" and "the opening of the Three Gates." Therefore the "Treatise on T'ai-chi ch'üan" says, "When the *wei-lü* is vertical, the spirit can reach the crown of the head." This process transforms the sexual energy (*ching*) into *ch'i* and the *ch'i* into spirit. Therefore it moves from the center of the bones. Bodhidharma's art, such as found in the *Sinew Changing Classic* and *Marrow Cleansing Classic*, places the highest value on *ch'i*. Here *ch'i* moves with the breath, rising along the *Jen* meridian in the front of the body to the head and face. This is hard *ch'i* and nothing else. It circulates only in the sinews and is not transformed into spirit. This is the external system.

T'ai-chi ch'üan is a system that also highly values *ch'i*. Just look at those passages in the "T'ai-chi ch'üan Classics" relating to *ch'i*: "Sink the *ch'i* to the *tan-t'ien*," "move the *ch'i* with the mind and the body with the *ch'i*," as well as, "pushing and pulling, back and forth, the *ch'i* sticks to the back," "the *ch'i* should be properly cultivated and not damaged," "the *ch'i* should be roused," "the *ch'i* is like a wheel," "the *ch'i* is like a nine-bends-pearl," "there is no place it does not benefit," "*ch'i* fills the entire body without the slightest blockage," and such expressions as, "When the mind and *ch'i* are masters, the bones and flesh obey," and "*ch'i* collects in the bones." At its highest, this is simply the function of "concentrating the *ch'i* and developing softness."

Now then, where should students begin to train their *ch'i*? What are the stages of progress and how can they

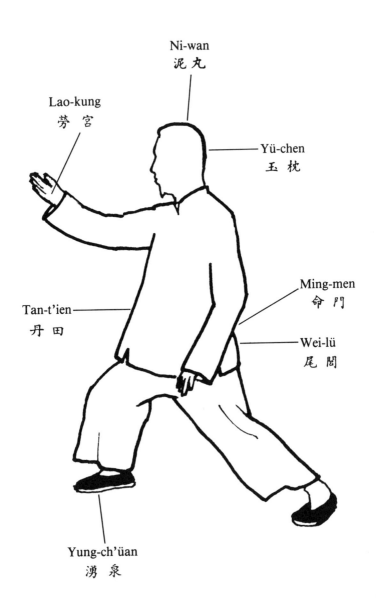

derive the full benefits? Let me give a general outline based on my own knowledge. The *ch'i* should sink to the *tan-t'ien*. The *tan-t'ien* is 1.3 inches below the navel in the abdomen, between the navel and the spine, but closer to the former by a ratio of 3:7. First draw the *ch'i* there with the mind. The *ch'i* should sink slowly and gradually, not too rapidly. If it descends too rapidly it will float back up. There is a four word formula which says: "Fine, long, calm, and slow." Once one has become adept, then any time and anywhere, by simply maintaining the mind and *ch'i* in the *tan-t'ien*, we will be obeying the command to "properly nourish and not harm" it. This is called, "When the mind and *ch'i* are masters, the bones and flesh obey." At this point the work of establishing our foundation is complete and we can now proceed step by step. First, we must pay attention to moving the *ch'i* with the mind, and the body with the *ch'i*, to rousing the *ch'i*, and to making the *ch'i* like a wheel. Then, in our give and take, back and forth, the *ch'i* should stick to the back. Next, we should seek to make the *ch'i* like a nine-beads-pearl and it will give benefit wherever it goes. Then the *ch'i* will fill the entire body without the slightest blockage. When it is called upon for use, then "the lower abdomen is completely relaxed and the *ch'i* is active." At the highest stage "the *ch'i* sinks and enters the bones and collects in the spine." At this level one has "concentrated the *ch'i* and developed softness and is like a child." If we speak of "transforming the *ch'i* into spirit," then we must go further and discuss how "the consciousness should be on the spirit and not on the *ch'i*. If it is on the *ch'i* there will be blocks. When there is *ch'i* there is no strength. Without *ch'i* one achieves essential hardness."

"*Ch'i*" is simply one word. But the word *ch'i* in the phrase, "transform sexual energy into *ch'i*," is somewhat different from the word *ch'i* in the expression, "the *ch'i* and blood." At this point the sexual energy *ch'i* is transformed into spirit and produces spiritual power. The power of *ch'i* cannot compare with it. This is what is meant by, "essential hardness is such that there is nothing it cannot smash." This is also called, "A high level of skill approaches the *tao*." Why stop at, "Wherever the hero goes, he has no match?"

Therefore what we mean by the "internal martial art" is based on the philosophical principles of the Yellow Emperor and Lao Tzu. When it comes to cultivating *ch'i* and regulating the breath, this is very difficult to describe. If one wishes to thoroughly understand it in all its details, this is exceptionally difficult without first understanding traditional Chinese medicine's *Yellow Emperor's Classic of Internal Medicine*. To measure it with modern medical principles, I'm afraid would only get one to the outer fence without ever glimpsing the secrets of the inner hall. Today's physicians know only about breathing, but do not know about *ch'i*. They know only about the diaphragm, but do not know about the *tan-t'ien*. They know only about tightening and relaxing, bending and extending of the muscles in movement, but do not know the function of the latent *ch'i* mechanism. They know only about the skeleton and joints, and that with training they can become strong, but do not know about changes within them resulting from the addition of sexual energy (*ching*) and nourishing the marrow. They know only about nervous sensation and the functioning of consciousness, but do not know the subtlety of reactions of the spirit. They know only about the circulation of the blood and cell metabolism, but do not know the principle of the mutual production and destruction of the Five Elements in the Five Viscera, or the complementary waxing and waning of *yin* and *yang*.

To summarize all of the above, let me just mention the most common ones and discuss them very generally. For example, let us take the distinctions among the various kinds of *ch'i*. There are actually three. First, within the body there is the *ch'i* of the blood. It is the most fundamental and maintains the body temperature at 37°C. Second, outside the body there is the air which enables the breath to reach the *tan-t'ien*. The *tan-t'ien* is the "sea of *ch'i*" and the "storehouse of sexual energy." If one cultivates *ch'i* for a long time and directs the breath to the *tan-t'ien*, this causes the sexual energy to be heated and to be transformed into *ch'i*. This is the third kind of *ch'i*. It is called Primordial *Ch'i*. This *ch'i* not only permeates every membrane of the body, but can penetrate into the bones. For a detailed discussion, see my *Thirteen Chapters*. The diaphragm is simply one vital mechanism in the functioning of *ch'i* and is only the expansion and contraction of muscle; yet the whole body consists of 656 major components. Without *ch'i* to propel it, the body would be nothing but a complex moving machine. The bones and joints of the body can be transformed into steel-like hardness. Without sexual energy *(ching)* and marrow to supplement and nourish them, they would become brittle and rotten: of what use would they be then? Nervous sensation and the function of consciousness would simply come to a halt without the reactions of the spirit to inspire them. Despite the blood circulation, cell metabolism and the presence of red and white corpuscles, without the full and empty aspects of the process of mutual production and destruction in the Five Viscera, there would be no complementary exchange of *yin* and *yang*.

To summarize all of the above, physicians do not study this in depth, and in fact are very skeptical. Since they are so skeptical, they should all the more diligently and deliberately seek to get to the bottom of it, and maintain a truly scientific attitude. I have yet to see anyone who carried out these two points. I cannot help but invite thorough study of the principles and applications of T'ai-chi ch'üan. It is consistent in all its aspects, internal and external, large and small, and it is relatively easy to observe the facts.

V. Three Introductory Chapters

From
*Master Cheng's
New Method
of Self-Study
for T'ai-chi ch'üan*

I. The Guiding Principle

The complete T'ai-chi ch'üan form consisted of more than one hundred and twenty movements. Among these there were many repetitions, executed over and over endlessly. This was a great waste of mental energy without any benefit to either theory or practice. I was very skeptical and hypothesized that this had but three functions. First, fearing that students lacked perseverance, they deliberately elaborated the form in order to extend the period of time and provide proper guidance. Second, they wanted the basic postures to be practiced repeatedly in order to guarantee the student's progress. Third, some felt that thirteen postures was too short and not adequate as an exercise. It is possible to raise these three points, but none are sufficiently persuasive. If a person lacks perseverance, it is not easy to make them persist, and they will give up whether the form is long or short. If there are certain basic important postures, they can be emphasized and practiced more often. If one is afraid that the form is too short, then there is nothing to prevent practicing it over and over again. I believe that the repetitions are excessive and have no significance. They waste mental energy and are without benefit. Therefore I often felt a desire to omit the complexities and simplify the form, and beginning with the easier postures progress to the more difficult. However, because of other responsibilities, I was unable to fulfill my desire for a long time.

In 1937 at the outbreak of the war with Japan, I served as head of the Hunan Martial Arts Academy and was in charge of training soldiers, policemen, students, and citizens. T'ai-chi ch'üan was a very important part of the curriculum. I had no choice but to simplify the form in order to make it more widely accessible. Only then could it have the effect of strengthening the race and the nation, of rousing the exhausted and raising the weak. Within a short time I received the enthusiastic endorsement of colleagues and students. This was the inspiration for the present book. Truly it is a case of adapting to need and not of creating something novel and difficult for its own sake. I hope that the worthy and wise men of all the world will forgive my shortcomings and offer suggestions for improvement.

II. Examining Roots and Branches

Master Yang Ch'eng-fu explained the main principles of T'ai-chi ch'üan as follows:

1. Whenever Master Yang lectured on the postures or sparring, he would tell us that in practicing T'ai-chi ch'üan, one does not move the hands. Moving the hands is not T'ai-chi ch'üan. He also admonished us by saying that his father, Chien-hou, would always quote the following passage from the *Classics* to his students: "From the feet to the legs to the waist should be one flow of *ch'i*," and also, "the root is

in the feet, it is developed in the legs, controlled by the waist, and applied through the hands and fingers." This means that the hands must follow and not move independently. Thus we can see that root and branch are never separated. Furthermore, the "Mental Elucidation" says at the very beginning, "Move the *ch'i* with the mind and the body with the *ch'i*," which also proves that the hands do not move independently. What defines T'ai-chi ch'üan as T'ai-chi ch'üan is that the inner and outer are one. To depart from this in speaking of T'ai-chi ch'üan is unthinkable.

2. "Sink the shoulders, drop the elbows, and 'sit the wrists.'" This means that the shoulders must neither rise nor cave in. The elbows must neither flap up nor be pressed down tightly. If both are natural, they will sink and drop. "Sitting" the wrists is a bit more difficult. It requires that the tendons in the back of the hand not stand out, or what is traditionally called "beautiful lady's hand." Only this will do. The fingers are not pressed tightly together nor are they spread out; they are not bent nor are they straight. Rather, within the open seek the closed, and within the bent seek the straight. Then it will be correct. It is especially important that the *ch'i* reaches the *lao-kung* point in the middle of the palm and then extends to the fingertips.

3. "Depress the chest and raise the back." Depress the chest means that one must not stick out the chest, but also not allow it to cave in. Rather, the chest should be relaxed. Only this is the correct method. Raising the back is not easily explained. It is a sign that the *ch'i* has passed through the "Three Gates." This will be explained in greater detail later.

4. "Sink the *ch'i* to the *tan-t'ien*." The *tan-t'ien* is in the abdomen located 1.3 inches below the navel and closer to the navel than the *ming-men* point in the spine. Sinking the *ch'i* means gathering the *ch'i* in the *tan-t'ien*. It does not mean

deliberately trying to make the abdomen "full." Be very careful of this.

5. "Cause the energy at the crown of the head to be light and sensitive." The head should not incline backwards nor hang forward. It should not wag to the left or right, but should be as if suspended from above. When this is supplemented by keeping the *wei-lü* vertical, the spirit extends to the crown of the head, that is, it reaches all the way to the *ni-wan* point.

6. The knees. When executing the Beginning posture, stand naturally, neither stiffly erect nor stooped. In Brush Knee Twist Step, Single Whip, and so forth, the knee must not extend beyond the foot and the instep should be as soft as cotton. Then the *yung-ch'üan* point will be able to relax and sink when it touches the ground.

All of the above points are extremely vital and have thus been specially outlined. I hope that students will give them a good deal of thought.

III. Respecting the Transmission

This book was written as a sequel to Master Yang Ch'eng-fu's *Complete Principles and Applications of T'ai-chi ch'üan* and is based on his teachings. However, his form is excessively long and there are very few students who persevere to the end, let alone maintain their practice over a long period. If we desire to guide them skillfully, we cannot but reduce complexity to simplicity and progress from the easy to the more difficult. I have therefore eliminated seventy per cent of the repetitions and have given this form the name Simplified T'ai-chi ch'üan. My senior fellow student, Ch'en Wei-ming, has praised it enthusiastically and encouraged me to publish it. It never occurred to him that I had violated our teacher's principles.

The Yang family taught this art for three generations to the imperial Manchu clan during the declining years of the [Ch'ing] dynasty, and therefore the people had no knowledge of it. With the founding of the Republic [1911], it gradually spread to Kiangsu and Chekiang. I began to apply myself to it because of a serious lung disorder. After a long time I was able to acquire the true transmission. Today, with the intention of sharing it with others, I have committed the oral teachings to book form. I want not only to strengthen our own race and nation, but enable its benefits to reach all of mankind. This is my great hope. The philosophical principles of this art's theory are superior and without equal. Not only are they applicable to the conduct of affairs in general, but they are especially relevant to military strategy. Despite my shortcomings, after twenty years of mental effort, I have set forth the main outline in thirteen chapters, and hence the title of my book is taken from this. I hope that students will pursue it faithfully and not leave off after they have achieved strength and health. Self-cultivation is the *tao* of long life and begins with this. It is vastly different from medicine which attempts to remedy imbalance with imbalance. If we compare it to meditation, it does not have the negative effect of wearing out the *ch'i* for the sake of easing the body. As Mr. Ts'ai Tzu-min has said, "T'ai-chi ch'üan can protect us from humiliation and preserve our life. It should be considered a national treasure that offers a hundred benefits and not a single harm. It should be a model for our 400 million countrymen." These are wise words, indeed.

VI.
The Three Kinds of Fearlessness

From
Master Cheng's
New Method
of Self-Study
for T'ai-chi ch'üan

Those who want to study T'ai-chi ch'üan usually have one of several motives. In general, there are those who are sick or weak and seek good health; there are those who study for self-defense, and those who are impressed by the subtlety of the art and seek its true principles. Apart from these, there are also people who have a passing fancy, who follow the crowd, as well as those who are simply lacking in perseverance. But these people do not even enter into the discussion. What I mean by "fearlessness" applies only to those who are willing to work.

1. Do not be afraid to work. If you are afraid of hard work, you have no hope of making progress. The "T'ai-chi ch'üan Classics" say that, "the root is in the feet." If one is afraid of hard work, the feet will never develop root. This is why there is no doubt that working the feet hard is

beneficial to the heart and brain. The basic method for beginners is to take three to five minutes in the morning and evening and alternately stand on one foot. Gradually increase the time and little by little sink deeper. Pay attention to sinking the *ch'i* to the *tan-t'ien* and to the sole of the foot sticking to the ground. Do not use the least bit of force. Standing in the "post" position, use your middle and index fingers to steady yourself against a chair or table so as to provide stability and balance. After some practice, eliminate the middle and use only the index finger to support yourself. After a time, you will develop greater stability and will be able to forego all support and naturally stand steadily. After this, use Raise Hands or Play Guitar to continue your standing practice. The posture Preparation is the best "post standing" practice for developing Primordial Unity, and Single Whip for opening the joints. Nothing is more valuable than these for both principles and applications. They cannot be overlooked.

2. Do not be afraid to take a loss. The secret transmissions of T'ai-chi ch'üan say, "Forget yourself and follow others." Does not forgetting yourself and following others involve taking a loss? Therefore, at the very beginning of my *Thirteen Chapters* I have said that we must learn to "invest in loss." How can this be learned? It is learned by allowing others to attack us and assail us, and not only not resisting, but not striking back. The most important thing is to stick, connect, adhere, and follow, and then we will be able to neutralize ever so lightly. This idea is impossible to grasp for those of shallow learning and brutish ways. How much more so those who are just beginning? Can they possibly avoid taking losses? If one is afraid of taking losses, it is better not to study at all. But those who are anxious to study can do no better than to begin by learning to invest in loss. Learning to invest in loss means not seeking easy short cuts. Those who seek small short cuts will take great losses. Conversely, those who invest in small losses will gain great short cuts. Those possessed of superior in-

telligence will certainly desire to receive the true principles and applications. Where should they begin? Did not Lao Tzu say, "Concentrate your *ch'i* and develop softness. Can you be like a child?" This is the watchword for T'ai-chi ch'üan. Students should begin their study with this. If they can concentrate their *ch'i* and develop softness, when it comes to learning the marvelous results of investing in loss, they will already have no fear of it. This is what the mnemonic verses call, "Let him attack me with tremendous force, while I use a pull of four ounces to deflect a thousand pounds." With this, one can be said to have already gained the effect of developing softness.

3. Do not be afraid of intimidation. This is what Lao Tzu called, "The rhinoceros will have no place to lodge his horn, the tiger no place to plant his claws, and the soldier no place to land his blade." Why is this? "Because he does not acknowledge death." He also says, "Nothing in the world is softer than water, but not even the strongest can overcome it," as well as, "The softest in the world will overtake the hardest." Now rhinoceroses, tigers, and weapons are the most intimidating things in the world, but he says that they are not worthy of their reputation. Instead, he praises weak water, which because of its extreme softness, none can overcome. This is what is called, "When I have no body, what harm can come to me." So even if attacked by the sharpness of weapons, claws, and horns, there is nothing to fear. If I am afraid, then there will be tension in my spirit and body. If I am tense, I will not be able to relax, and if I am unable to relax, how can I be soft? To not be soft means to be hard. So those who really get to the heart of T'ai-chi ch'üan theory have the spirit of great fearlessness. This is also similar to Mencius saying that, "Mount T'ai could collapse in front of you, but your complexion would not change" and "I excel at cultivating my great *ch'i*." This is also what Lao Tzu meant by, "concentrating one's *ch'i* and developing softness." What intimidation is there to fear?

VII. Eliminating the Three Faults

From
*Master Cheng's
New Method
of Self-Study
for T'ai-chi ch'üan*

I have written this book especially for those who are limited by busy work schedules and for women who are occupied with household responsibilities, in other words, for the benefit of those who cannot study with teachers. It is much simpler than correspondence study. The emphasis here is only on teaching the fine points of the form postures. Thus it leans for the most part towards principles. Originally, T'ai-chi ch'üan was based on the idea that where there are principles, practice must follow. If one desires to pursue this in great depth, refer later to my book in English, *Tai Chi Chuan: A Simplified Method of Calisthenics for Health and Self-Defense* and my *Master Cheng's Thirteen Chapters on T'ai-chi ch'üan* in Chinese for a clearer understanding. At the outset of self-study, one must first strive to eliminate three faults. In my forty years experience, those who are able to eliminate these three faults and study faithfully are assured of enjoying the rewards they seek. As for people who are slightly less gifted, it simply means making a bit more of an effort. Everybody is aware of these faults and the remedy is simple and readily at hand. Most often it is a case of persisting in bad habits and an unwillingness to rectify them. In my youth, I too was guilty of this, and that is why I am able to speak with such authority. Let me elaborate.

The first fault is lack of perseverance. This is what Confucius was referring to when he said, "A man who lacks perseverance cannot be a witch doctor." The medical practice of shamans is not an orthodox art, but without perseverance even this is impossible. How much more so T'ai-chi ch'üan which leads us from philosophy to science. T'ai-chi ch'üan's principles of "using softness to overcome hardness" and "concentrating the *ch'i* and developing softness" are based on the philosophical concepts of the *I ching,* Yellow Emperor and Lao Tzu. When it comes to actually putting into practice "using a pull of four ounces to deflect a thousand pounds," this is what would be called a "jack" in science, or what is commonly referred to as "uncheckable pressure" in mechanics. This then is the crystallization of philosophy and science. I firmly believe that it can serve as a bridge between Chinese and Western culture. However, are principles and applications the only benefit? If one approaches the study of this art without perseverance, not only is it a waste of time, but one emerges empty-handed from a mountain of treasures. Is this not a great pity?

I often regret my lack of perseverance as a young man. Because of my poor health, I took up martial arts many times, but as soon as I made a bit of progress, I would abandon them. Finally, thirty-nine years ago, I contracted a difficult case of tuberculosis. Once again I took up T'ai-chi ch'üan and fully recovered. Thereupon I determined to never give up my practice again. At that time I took all the postures in the form, and using the quickest method of practice, did a whole round in six or seven minutes. Morning and evening I did just one form, seeking only to keep up my regimen without lapsing. Actually, at the time I was very busy with teaching and other school responsibilities and had no free time even for self-study. But from this period on, before long I had made progress. In the morning immediately after rising, I would not wash or eat without first doing a form; in the evening before sleeping, I would not go to bed without also doing a form. After a long time this became habitual and I never again quit. The idea is that the greatest joy in life lies in helping others, and we should not be afraid to make sacrifices. Now if I desire health, but lack perseverance in spending just a few minutes morning and evening, then how dare I set myself up as an example to others? Therefore, I was ashamed of my foolishness and determined to correct this fault.

The second fault is greediness. Hence the saying, "If one is greedy nothing can be thoroughly chewed" and Lao Tzu's "Have little and receive much; have much and be confused" are true indeed. When I was young I had an older friend, Lu Chien, styled Ch'eng-pei, who was a native of Yü-yao County, Chekiang. He had travelled to Yen-tang and before returning home stopped by and said, "In former times, when gentlemen were about to take their leave, they offered some parting words. I would like to leave you with this advice. The Cheng family excels in three fields. If you take these up faithfully, there is no doubt the line will continue. But if you are greedy and attempt to learn everything, I'm afraid you will amount to little. Listen to my advice and confine yourself to poetry, calligraphy, and painting." I did follow it. This old man was a very useful friend, and if I have accomplished anything, it is all due to him. I can never forget it.

The *I ching* says, "By making it easy, it is easily understood; by making it simple, it is simply followed." Practicing T'ai-chi ch'üan is no different. If one is taught a posture or two today, quietly concentrate, then polish and memorize it. Only then can something be gained. Otherwise confusion is inevitable. In the spring of 1938, while I was head of the Hunan Martial Arts Academy, the whole province was caught up in the martial arts movement. Regardless of age or sex, everyone had an opportunity to study. I wanted to popularize T'ai-chi ch'üan, and therefore every two months I personally taught some forty people, the heads and teachers of martial arts schools from every county in the province who were sent for training. Because of the limited time, I decided to make certain abbreviations in the form in order to simplify it. Originally T'ai-chi ch'üan had only thirteen postures, but after long transmission, the number of postures increased. It required a great deal of time to practice and could not easily be popularized. For this reason I reduced the number to thirty-seven, or twenty-four more than the original thirteen. This is adapting to the times. However do not take my "Simplified T'ai-chi ch'üan" to be simple.

After victory in the War of Resistance Against Japan, I took this manuscript to Shanghai and discussed it with senior fellow student, Ch'en Wei-ming, who praised it greatly and said he agreed with me completely. He immediately wrote a preface to express his admiration. Ch'en Wei-ming is a scholar and a gentleman and would never engage in insincere flattery. Nevertheless, there are some ignorant individuals who disagree with my action and do not realize the great pains I have taken to propagate what might otherwise have become a lost art. There is nothing more I can say to them.

The third fault is haste. The saying that haste makes waste is wise advice indeed. Try to remember that as water flows it naturally cuts a channel, and that things cannot be forced. The ancients often said of the arts that we must steep ourselves in rich beauty and thoroughly savor it. They also said that difficulties will eventually disappear like melting ice, and everything will make perfect sense. I believe that we must practice T'ai-chi ch'üan with this attitude. Moreover, this art includes both principles and practice, with equal attention to mind and hand, and requires that we grasp the philosophical concepts as well as master the scientific applications. Then the profit will be infinite. In summary, if we can systematically eliminate these three faults, then we can make successful progress without any obstacles whatsoever.

VIII.
On What I Have Gained from Study

From
*Master Cheng's
New Method
of Self-Study
for T'ai-chi ch'üan*

More than ten years ago a student asked me, "Sir, you are a master of five arts. Which has been the most satisfying to you personally to teach?" I answered that teaching T'ai-chi ch'üan was the most enjoyable. Those who had heard this were very skeptical and asked if it was not a bit unrefined and brutish. I responded that they did not really understand, and that T'ai-chi ch'üan was the essence of the philosophy of life. As for the achievement of true excellence in T'ai-chi ch'üan, there is no art more difficult. Absolutely no ordinary martial art can compare with it.

They asked to learn more about it. I said that when I was a young man, I taught poetry, calligraphy, and painting, deriving the greatest pleasure from teaching calligraphy because it offered the benefits of a strengthening exercise. During the years of early manhood I was uprooted and made my way to Szechwan where I earned a living as a physician. Unexpectedly, my success as a doctor was tremendous, and everyone said I was a great saviour. As a result, my eating and sleeping habits became irregular and I suffered unspeakably. Moreover, all my days were spent face to face with knit brows and suffering countenances. Beset with life and death pleas, could I greet them with a smile? I had no choice but to see them. Only teaching T'ai-chi ch'üan could eliminate illness, confer long life, and gladden heart and spirit. Young and old can come together and share the benefits. One can emulte Lao Lai-tzu, who played like a child even in his seventies, and not grow weary in old age, thus rising above the cruel game of nature. To "concentrate one's *ch'i* and develop softness" truly can be said to bestow infinite health and happiness.

If you ask me what I have gained from forty years of study, it can be summed up in twelve words: "Swallow the *ch'i* of Heaven; receive the earth's strength; longevity through softness." If you ask its usefulness, then I would answer that in the human body, *ch'i* leads the blood. Therefore, if the *ch'i* flourishes, then the blood flourishes. Heaven is rich in great *ch'i*. To avail oneself of much of it cannot be considered greedy. Strength is very useful in the human body. The earth is valued for its supporting power. If we can receive just a tiny bit ot it, the usefulness will be infinite. If one can develop softness, then as Lao Tzu says, one can be like a child. In this way, our life has no limit. The three phrases mentioned above represent the Three Powers [Heaven, earth and man] in the human body. The highest position receives the *ch'i* of Heaven, that is, the *ni-wan* point at the crown of the head. This can increase our spiritual *ch'i*. The lowest position is earth. If we receive the strength of the earth, then the important *yung-ch'üan* point in the ball of the foot will increase in rooting power. The center is occupied by the important *tan-t'ien* point located in the abdomen in line with the waist. If one can concentrate the *ch'i* and develop softness, then the waist will become lively and flexible, the *ch'i* of the kidneys will be abundant, and we can extend our lives.

The method of practicing this is extremely simple. First, whenever you have a spare moment, feel as if your *ni-wan* point is holding up Heaven, absorb Heaven's *ch'i* and sink it to the *tan-t'ien*. Second, when you are in the midst of activity, sitting, or just standing about and there is an opportunity to really pay attention, then use the sole of the foot to stick to the earth and imagine that it is sinking into the earth. After a long time imagine that the power of your foot is connected to the gravitational pull of the earth. If you can do this, then the foot will possess root. Third, the ancients referred to the *tan-t'ien* in these words, "Walking, sitting, retiring, or sleeping, you just can't get away from it." The most important thing is to keep the mind and *ch'i* in the *tan-t'ien*, just like a hen incubating her eggs. This is what is meant by "knowledge arriving at the highest good." The *tao* cannot be forsaken for a single instant. If it can, it is not the true *tao*. This is also what Mencius meant when he referred to "my great *ch'i*." All of this means never leaving the *tan-t'ien*. If even this little bit of what I have learned is conscientiously put into practice, it absolutely cannot be matched by any casual exercise. Health and longevity then become a simple matter.

IX.
Dialogue with Disciples on Questions Concerning the "Treatise on T'ai-chi ch'üan"*

From
Thirteen Chapters
and *New Method*
of Self-Study

Section One

Question 1. When they say, "The *ch'i* should be roused and the spirit concentrated within" and "Move the *ch'i* with the mind and the body with the *ch'i*" does that mean that the internal and external are in balance, and that therein lies the unity of movement and stillness? Please explain more fully.
Answer. This is a good question! Mobilizing the *ch'i* to move the body is the root, the internal; rousing the *ch'i* is the branch, the external. Concentrating within is stillness; rousing is movement. The two can be in balance and unite as one. But "rousing" is not just rousing one's own *ch'i*, it means rousing one's own *ch'i* and the *ch'i* of Heaven and earth. Only then can we accomplish great things.

Question 2. "Cause there to be no deficiencies, no hollows or protrusions, and no discontinuities." This corresponds perfectly with your chapter on energy and physics where you say, "unbroken continuity, round and round without end, circular and open, infinite and inexhaustible." Please tell me if I am correct or not.

Answer. Your comparison is very apt, but even better is the "Treatise's" saying, "Stand like a balance and move like a wheel." This allows the greatest facility.

Question 3: "The root is in the feet, it is developed in the legs, controlled by the waist and applied through the hands and fingers." This principle has already been fully discussed in your chapter on the stages of development in T'ai-chi ch'üan under phases two and three of the stage of man. It is just that I do not understand how the feet and hands move at the same time.

Answer. This is an excellent question! What we mean by "rooted in the feet and applied through the hands" refers to one unbroken flow of energy. The principal and application are obvious and easily observable. Just look at a person as they issue energy. When the *ch'i* arrives, the job is done. There can be absolutely no instability in the root. Furthermore, the right foot and left hand and the left foot and the right hand must be connected in a single flow.

Question 4. "Seizing the opportunity and gaining the power advantage" is the highest level of interpreting energy. You have explained this in detail in your chapter on the stages of development in T'ai-chi ch'üan under phase two of the stage of Heaven. It is just that I have difficulty in understanding how to practice its application. Can you give me some examples that might help explain it?

Answer. If you refer to my note to number 9 in the chapter on Master Yang Ch'eng-fu's oral transmissions you will understand it easily.

Question 5. "If there is an above, there must be a below; if there is a front, there must be a behind; if there is a left there must be a right." I learned this from your chapter on energy and physics when you discussed the operation of levers. Can you add anything to this?
Answer. Regardless of the circumstances, theory and practice remain absolutely consistent.

Question 6. "To raise something up, apply breaking power. Then its root will naturally break and it will certainly be swiftly repelled." Is this what is meant by uprooting energy?
Answer. Yes, raising means to use uprooting energy. But strength is not sufficient to uproot someone. Therefore we add breaking. To grasp my idea, you might compare it to jumping. If you want to jump, you must first crouch, and then you will have the power. This is precisely the same as the concept in physics of energy being the product of strength, speed and time.

Question 7. "In movement they separate; in stillness they unite." What is the difference between separating and uniting, bending and extending, opening and closing?
Answer. Uniting in stillness and separating in movement is the essence of T'ai-chi. As for opening and closing, these refer to the body and *ch'i*. Therefore, when the body opens, the *ch'i* closes; when the body closes, the *ch'i* opens. Bending and extending are similar in meaning to opening and closing.

Section Two
Question 1. "The opponent is hard while I am soft. This is called neutralizing. I follow the opponent's back. This is called sticking." I already understand the marvelous applications of hardness and softness, but what can you tell me about "following the back" and "sticking?"
Answer. "Forgetting oneself and following others" is what is meant by following. In other words, if the opponent does

not move, I do not move. The opponent cannot fathom me. Giving an opponent the slightest opportunity is called the "back." When the opponent makes the least move, I anticipate it by moving first. Knowing that the opponent offers an opportunity to be exploited, I come to the fore, while he falls to the rear. This is what we mean by the "back." This comes from listening to energy and is impossible without sticking.

Question 2. "From practice one gradually awakens to interpreting energy, and from interpreting energy, by degrees, one reaches perfect clarity." You have already fully discussed this in your chapter on the stages of development under phases two and three of the stage of Heaven. Apart from this, do you have anything to add?
Answer. You have spoken well. There is nothing to add.

Question 3. What is meant by, "If weight is applied to the left, become empty on the left; if weight is applied on the right, become quiet on the right?"
Answer. This is an application. If someone pushes me on the left, then I empty the left. It is the same on the right. "Quiet" means empty. From the point of view of one's own body, of course, this is not true.

Question 4. What is meant by, "A feather cannot be added, nor a fly alight?"
Answer. When sparring, apart from sticking and joining, if the opponent wants to issue energy against me, I will not accept even a fly or feather's weight.

---

* Translators note: Section 1 refers to the "Treatise on T'ai-chi ch'üan" attributed to Chang San-feng and Section 2 refers to the "Treatise on T'ai-chi ch'üan" attributed to Wang Tsung-yüeh.

X.
Questions and Answers Concerning the "Mental Elucidation of the Thirteen Postures"

From
Thirteen Chapters
and *New Method of Self-Study*

Question 1. Is there any difference between the statements: "Move the *ch'i* with the mind and direct it to sink. Then it is able to collect in the bones." and, "The spirit should gather within and then it collects in the spine?"

Answer. Although the idea of gathering is the same, spirit and *ch'i* are different. When the spirit gathers, then the will is not scattered. The *ch'i* gathering in the bones is the foundation of the principles of "without *ch'i* there is essential hardness," "energy moves like steel tempered a hundred times," and so forth.

Question 2. "When issuing energy you must sink and relax." How can one be relaxed at the moment of issuing energy?

Answer. Sinking describes my own internal state. Relaxing is the manner of application used against an opponent. This is what is meant by "repelling an opponent like an arrow leaving the bowstring." It is clear and decisive, not like clumsily dragging mud and hauling water.

Question 3. "Strength issues from the spine. Steps follow changes of the body." Does this strength which issues from the spine correspond with the idea of the *Jen* and *Tu* meridians which you discussed in your chapter on the equal importance of the heart and spine? Does "steps follow changes in the body" have the same meaning as "the controlling mechanism is in the waist?"

Answer. The word "strength" (*li*) which you are quoting from the passage, "strength issues from the back" should actually be the word "energy" (*chin*). Issuing from the back relies on the strength of the spine, or what is called, "store energy like drawing a bow." Your statement that, "steps follow changes in the body," relating to the waist being in control, is quite correct.

Question 4. In the statement, "Gathering is issuing. Break and reconnect," "gathering" expresses the idea of uprooting, but what is meant by "Break and reconnect?"

Answer. "Breaking" is in the physical body; "connecting" is in the consciousness. This is similar to the two sayings: "The lotus root breaks but the fibers remain intact" and "The brush stops writing but the idea goes on."

Question 5. Please explain more fully the statement: "In moving in and out one must use plaiting and folding; in advancing and retreating one must use turning and changing steps."

Answer. The method of plaiting and folding up is a secret transmission I learned from the Yang family. It consists of plaiting and folding up the three joints—shoulders, elbows and wrists—and coordinating this with advancing, retreating, turning, and changing steps. The transformations of moving in and out are truly infinite.

Question 6. "The consciousness of the whole body should be on the spirit and not on the *ch'i*. If it is on the *ch'i* there will be blocks. If there is *ch'i* there is no strength. Without *ch'i* one achieves essential hardness." When I first read this passage I was extremely skeptical. However, as soon as I read your chapter on the stages of development under phase three of the stage of Heaven, then it all became perfectly clear. Is there anything else you would like to add?
Answer. You have the basic idea.

XI. Questions on the "Song of the Thirteen Postures"

From *Thirteen Chapters* and *New Method of Self-Study*

Question 1. Does the statement, "When one is roused from stillness by movement, one's movement should be like stillness. Follow the opponent's changes, expressing perfect spiritual composure," mean the same as, "Respond to movement with stillness and move as if in stillness?" What is meant by "expressing perfect spiritual composure?"

Answer. Without stillness one cannot gauge the opponent's changes. We freely allow him to change, but are able to control him with stillness. This is what is meant by "perfect spiritual composure."

Question 2. Is the phenomenon of *ch'i* rising up when the belly is relaxed the same as your explanation of directing *ch'i* from the *tan-t'ien* in your chapter on the stages of development under the third phase of the stage of the earth?

Answer. No. This is the result of expelling *ch'i* when issuing energy. Therefore, when issuing energy, you must not hold the breath. If you do so, you will suffer internal injury. One should exhale with a loud sound and the *ch'i* will rise up with the energy.

XII. Questions on the "Song of Push-Hands"

From
Thirteen Chapters
and *New Method
of Self-Study*

Question 1. "Ward-off, Roll-back, Press, and Push must be executed correctly." What is really meant by "correctly?"
Answer. See my note to number 11 in the chapter on oral transmissions. It is discussed in detail there.

Question 2. You have already fully explained the concept of deflecting with four ounces and repelling a thousand pounds in your note to number 12 in your chapter on the secret oral trnsmissions. Is there anything to be added?
Answer. There is nothing else.

Question 3. In the statement, "Draw the opponent in, cause him to land on nothing, gather together and repel. Stick, connect, adhere, and follow. Do not break or resist," does the phrase, "gather together and repel" mean storing energy and then issuing it? What about "breaking" and "resisting?"

Answer. This has to do with uprooting. "Breaking" means actually disconnecting; "resisting" means forceful energy. Both of these are the opposite of sticking and following. This results from ego and the inability to give up ourselves and follow others.

XIII. Important Points for Self-Study

From
*Master Cheng's
New Method
of Self-Study
for T'ai-chi ch'üan*

When practicing the postures, always remember these two important phrases: "When moving everything moves; when at rest everything is at rest." It is especially important to be aware that the "root is in the feet," and that the weight of the whole body must rest on one leg. "The waist is the controller" means that not only the hands and feet follow the turning of the waist, but from the top of the head to the very heels, including the vision, all must follow the waist. Traditionally, it is said, "When practicing T'ai-chi ch'üan, the hands do not move." This means that the hands and feet do not move independently, but that the waist rules.

"When the *wei-lü* is vertical, the spirit can reach the crown of the head" and "The whole body is light and nimble, as if suspended from above." These two statements must not be neglected. If one's head wobbles, then as the secret transmission states, "even if you study for thirty years you will fail." Thus, if the *wei-lü* is not vertical, the spirit cannot reach the crown of the head. Holding the head as if suspended from above is like braiding the hair in a queue and tying it to a rafter.

"Every point on the body is capable of being full or empty, and the body as a whole has its full and empty aspect." Without full and empty there can be no *yin* and *yang*. Without *yin* and *yang*, there is no T'ai-chi. For example, the two hands must be distinguished according to *yin* and *yang*; *yin* and *yang*, of course, means full and empty. The same is true for the feet. However, the left hand corresponds to the right foot and the right hand to the left foot. This is because of the diagonal cross-over of the nervous system. This is the division of full and empty with respect to left and right, above and below, hands and feet. What is meant by "the body as a whole has its full and empty aspect" is that the root is in the feet and that the weight of the whole body should rest on just one foot. If both feet use strength at the same time, this is double-weightedness. Being double-weighted is like the Shaolin "horse stance." This is the greatest error to be avoided in T'ai-chi ch'üan. Remember this well!

"Every joint in the body should be interconnected; then the *ch'i* can flow." The flow of *ch'i* is not only beneficial to the body, but very useful as well. Issuing energy and uprooting both rely on the interconnectedness of all the joints in the body to accomplish the "lever" function, as it is known in mechanics. Otherwise all the limbs and joints will be uncoordinated and unable to respond to our will in dealing with situations.

"The *ch'i* should be roused. That is, the *ch'i* in the *tan-t'ien* and the air are mutually roused." Some time ago I expounded the theory of "swimming on dry land." (Refer to my *Thirteen Chapters* where I compare air to water.) Gradually as one moves back and forth and rotates the body, one will feel pressure. After a long time, the pressure will become tremendous. This is what is known as, "Where there is emptiness, fill it." Then when sparring with a very strong opponent, one will feel as if pushing the air. This is known as, "Where there is fullness, empty it." When you have mastered this, it will prove infinitely useful.

"Concentrate your spirit within and express total calm without." This is how one achieves perfection in both principle and practice. "Mount T'ai could collapse in front of us and a deer suddenly appear on our right, but our complexion would not change or even an eye blink." This is because the spirit is concentrated within and one has developed imperturbability. It is simply the function of what Mencius meant by "cultivating my great *ch'i*." "Long Boxing" is like long rivers and great seas, flowing on and on without end." T'ai-chi ch'üan originally was "Thirteen Postures Long Boxing." This is because its movements flow on and on without end. But movement must have its controlling force in order to produce impetus, just like a train, automobile, or trolley. First there is mobilization and then movement. The excess energy left over from movement then swings back. This is what the *I ching* calls, "hard and soft replace each other and the eight trigrams alternate in succession." This, too, is movement and swing. At the end of every movement there must be a swing, and before the end of each swing a new movement begins. Round and round without end, forever in perpetual motion. Therefore, although T'ai-chi ch'üan has only thirteen postures, it is still called Long Boxing. The idea is simply that, "like long rivers and great seas, it flows on and on without end," or the principle of what the *I ching* calls, "exchanging and succeeding." This, then, is the movement and swing of Heaven and earth, *yin* and *yang*; it is endless. This has nothing to do with the length of the posture stances. Even if you increase the number of postures to ten thousand, this is irrelevant and not worthy of being called, "flowing on and on without end; this phrase was intended to describe uninterrupted continuity and nothing else.

The three words, "mind is ruler" is the single most important formula in T'ai-chi ch'üan. "Move the *ch'i* with the mind and the body with the *ch'i*." This provides the impetus. The hands and feet absolutely must not move independently, but rather follow the waist. This is why it is said, "In practicing T'ai-chi ch'üan the hands do not move." Moreover, the feet also do not move of themselves. Therefore, the movements in T'ai-chi ch'üan truly deserve to be described as, "If one hair is pulled, the whole body is set in motion." Students must experience this for themselves and then they will grasp it.

XIV. Afterword to *Thirteen Chapters*

From
Thirteen Chapters

Students of T'ai-chi ch'üan must first understand the significance of principles and applications. Before discussing practical applications, we must first devote ourselves to principles. Principles are the root; applications the branches. When the principles are fully grasped, then the applications can be mastered. How much more important for those who seek spiritual enlightenment and immortality? My chapter on energy and physics should facilitate understanding for beginning students. The remainder of the book is based on the original principles of T'ai-chi ch'üan. Fearing that students might still find it difficult to understand these esoteric secrets, allow me to cite some further examples from physiology as proof.

What T'ai-chi ch'üan calls the "*tan-t'ien*" is what the Taoists call "the one and only method." The *tan-t'ien* is located in the abdomen, closer to the navel. This is what in physiology is called, "the body's center of gravity," located along the line of the waist. Its position and significance is precisely the same as that of the *tan-t'ien*. The center of gravity is also what T'ai-chi ch'üan calls "central equilibrium." Central equilibrium cannot be saparated from the *tan-t'ien*. This is why the *Classics* say, "At all times keep the waist in mind," "the waist is the ruler," and "the waist is the pivot." In other words, we can say that T'ai-chi ch'üan is an exercise which emphasizes man's center of gravity. The *Classics* say, "Stand like a balance and you can control the eight directions" and "erect and relaxed without leaning or inclining." These express the idea of striving for balance and vertical posture in order not to lose one's center of gravity.

Apart from the *tan-t'ien*, the most important points that T'ai-chi ch'üan stresses are, "When the *wei-lü* is vertical, the spirit can rise to the crown of the head" and "Cause the energy at the crown of the head to be light and sensitive." These two sentences contain an extremely critical principle. "When the *wei-lü* is vertical, the spirit can rise to the crown of the head" refers to the *wei-lü* and the *ni-wan* point on the crown of the head. As for "causing the energy at the crown of the head to be light and sensitive," this ability has to do with the point in the neck called the *yü-chen* [Jade Pillow]. This explains what the Taoists mean by "opening the Three Gates." The Three Gates are the *wei-lü, yü-chen,* and *ni-wan*. In physiology these Three Gates are called the parasympathetic nervous system. Its position is precisely the same as the *wei-lü, yü-chen,* and *ni-wan*. What is called the sympathetic nervous system refers to the spine. The sympathetic nervous system controls energy expenditure and the parasympathetic nervous system controls energy restoration. How are we able to restore expended energy? The explanation has to do with the diaphragm withdrawing and the thoracic cavity expanding downward, thus exerting pressure on the abdominal organs and stimulating the parasympathetic system. This in turn tends to slow the breathing and pulse and to increase the saliva, to decrease the blood sugar and lower the blood pressure, as well as improving urination and dispelling heat. All of this comes from sinking the *ch'i* to the *tan-t'ien*, keeping the *wei-lü* vertical, and causing the spirit to rise to the crown of the head. On the basis of the preceding two paragraphs, those who are able to understand physiology are ready to hear the *tao* of self-cultivation.

Next we must consider the question of physiological transformations. For example, let us discuss women. Fifty years ago the lives of Chinese women were confined to the home. They were restricted by a multitude of proprieties, such as, "men and women should not touch" and "reports of the man's world outside should not reach the women's quarters and reports of the women's world inside should not leave the women's quarters." Foot binding and breast binding were especially damaging to the body. Today's women have not only liberated their feet and breasts, but participate in gymnastics, high jumping, swimming, ball games, ballroom dancing, and social service, just as men do. However, looking at men and women, they are really miles apart. Weighing the advantages and disadvantages of equal participation, the latter predominate, as the former are by no means certain.

A woman's body by nature is dominated by the element blood. Tranquility is best suited to the cultivation of blood. This is completely different from *ch'i*. The former is primarily yielding and patient. If restricted to the inner chambers, women become depressed and melancholy, the blood becomes cold or even blocked, and illness may result. Modern women, however, are excessively active and their blood becomes easily depleted. This is like water which is heated to boiling. The result is the drying up of the menses and consumption. This is truly a case of excess being as dangerous as insufficiency. I believe that the strength or weakness of a nation or people is bound up with the sufficiency or insufficiency of the physical strength of its women. When women's physical strength is sufficient, then mothers will be productive and offspring strong; if it is insufficient, mothers will be sickly and their offspring weak. We might compare this to planting seeds. If the soil is fertile, there will be an abundant harvest, but if the soil is barren, the harvest will be meager. Looking at the question in this way, women must not be without exercise, but at the same time, it must not be overly strenuous. Regardless of age, nothing is better than T'ai-chi ch'üan for those who desire strength and good health. T'ai-chi ch'üan emphasizes softness, stillness, lightness, and subtlety. Thus it is far more suited to women than any other exercise. I, Cheng Man-ch'ing, wrote this book with a physician's sense of self-sacrificing dedication and a prime minister's responsibility to guide and uplift the people. Now I simply await those of keen perception to take advantage of it.

XV.
Afterword to *New Method of Self-Study*

From
*Master Cheng's
New Method
of Self-Study
for T'ai-chi ch'üan*

Sixty to seventy per cent of those who study T'ai-chi ch'üan quickly learn the form and feel that they have finished. They are sporadic in their practice and may even leave off study altogether. They come away empty handed from a mountain of riches. T'ai-chi ch'üan may indeed be justly called the means to "changing the bones into golden elixir." However, this is not accomplished by swallowing a golden elixir pill. The *I ching* says, "The movement of Heaven is powerful. The superior man strengthens himself unceasingly." This means that man should strive to strengthen himself and never give up. Then he will match the power of Heaven's movement. In this way, those who study T'ai-chi ch'üan will be able to reap the benefits of "changing the bones into golden elixir." Therefore, among my three hopes, the first is perseverance.

Thirty years ago in my Afterword to the *Thirteen Chapters*, I made special mention of T'ai-chi ch'üan as the most appropriate exercise for women and, in fact, their needing it even more than men. You are invited to refer to that work for details. I have stated in the past that T'ai-chi ch'üan is better able to reform one's disposition than any other exercise. Parents who are concerned about the health of their children should encourage it in the home and the children will be influenced quite unconsciously and naturally enjoy practicing. Not only is it a panacea for health, but without realizing it, the emotions are harmonized and the disposition is molded. Some time ago I wrote a poem, one line of which went, "Where can I find a tongue great enough to sing the praises of T'ai-chi ch'üan?" This simply expresses the idea of Vimalikirti's sympathy for the sick and Confucius' capacity for empathy.

PART TWO

XVI. Advanced Form Instructions

From
Thirteen Chapters
and *New Method
of Self-Study*

Posture 1
Preparation

This is the Preparation posture in the T'ai-chi ch'üan form. It is the same as the standing meditation posture known as Undifferentiated Unity (*hun-yüan*). With body held erect, first shift the weight to the right leg, bend it slightly and sit with the full weight on it. [The left leg is now empty with the heel raised. At the same time, the two wrists and elbows are raised two or three inches, or slightly bowed. This enables the *ch'i* to extend to the *lao-kung* point in the middle of the palm of the left hand, which correlates with the right foot, the two being connected by the same nerve channels.] Lift the left foot and step out to the left. Shift the weight to the left foot, raise the toes of the right foot and point them directly forward. At the same time, the

two elbows bend slightly with the backs of the wrists facing forward and slightly bent. The palms face down, slightly open. The tips of the fingers are slightly raised, pointing forward, neither spread apart nor pressed together.

Stand still with the head erect and vision straight ahead. The vision should be focused inwardly. The hearing should concentrate on the breath. The tongue sticks to the upper palate. Keep the mouth closed with lips touching. Sink the shoulders and allow the elbows to hang. Relax the chest and sink the *ch'i* to the *tan-t'ien*. When moving the *ch'i*, it should be fine, long, calm, and slow. This is the image of T'ai-chi [the Great Ultimate] before the separation of *yin* and *yang*. Both the inner and outer should be relaxed and open. The whole body should be released and completely natural. From the *wei-lü* point to the crown of the head there should be a feeling of connectedness, as if suspended from above. Maintain your stillness as if waiting for an opponent to make the first move. In this way the inner and outer are one, essence and function complete. Most people overlook the importance of this posture without realizing that it is the foundation for all the methods of training and application. Our practice must begin with a clear understanding of this posture.

Posture 2
Beginning

In the Beginning posture the hands rise. This represents T'ai-chi's giving birth to the "two aspects," which are *yin* and *yang*. *Yin* is form. On the lower plane it is the earth and therefore does not move. *Yang* is *ch'i*. On the higher plane it is Heaven and, as it is light and pure, tends to float upward. Therefore, at the beginning of our form, we mobilize the *ch'i* with the mind and sink it to the *tan-t'ien*.

When the *ch'i* is full within, the two hands float upward along with the *ch'i*. This then is what is meant by moving the body with the *ch'i*. This illustrates that when the *ch'i* is concentrated, the body opens outward. As the hands descend there is a reverse effect. When the body is unified the *ch'i* expands. Throughout the rest of the form, mobilizing the *ch'i* and moving the body, floating, sinking, opening and closing are all based on this.

The key to this movement lies in relaxing the wrist joint. Altogether the wrist undergoes six changes. From Stand Erect to Preparation is the first change. From Preparation to Beginning the two arms rise with the backs of the wrists leading the movement as if floating up from under water, fingers hanging down. This is the second change. When the two wrists rise to shoulder level, then once again direct the *ch'i* to extend the fingers. The sinews of the hand should appear neither too tight nor too lax. This is the third change. When drawing the hands back, the wrists and elbows fold in until the hands reach the point where the chest and armpits meet. During this movement the fingers hang down again. This is the fourth change. When the two hands are about to descend again, the wrists look as if they were sinking in water and the fingertips as if they were floating. This is the fifth change. When the two hands reach their original position at the sides of the body, this is the same as the Preparation posture, and is the sixth change. This is why I say that the Beginning posture emphasizes the movement of the hands and wrists.

Posture 3
Grasp Sparrow's Tail, Ward-off, Left

Grasp Sparrow's Tail is similar to the gesture known as "lifting up the cow's tail" in ancient Chinese dance. It is the collective name for the four postures: Ward-off, Roll-back, Press and Push. It also contains all the basic techniques in T'ai-chi ch'üan. In Push-hands we use the principle of "stick, connect, join and follow," "not losing contact when retreating and not using force when advancing" and "back and forth continuous motion." We compare the arms to a sparrow's tail which the Push-hands partners grasp alternately.

Ward-off, Left continues from the end of the Beginning posture. If an opponent directly facing me attempts to strike the right side of my chest with his right fist, I immediately sit into my left foot and allow the right side of my chest to open by turning my waist to the right. Simultaneously the right foot turns out to the right. The right hand is raised to the level of the armpit in order to make contact with the opponent's wrist. The palm of the right hand should face down. The palm of the left hand faces up at hip level as if holding an object with two hands. Our eyes focus forward in preparation for adopting an offensive posture.

At this point, the opponent realizes he has been neutralized and will certainly attempt to withdraw his right fist. By the time he throws his left fist, I am already sitting on my right foot and with my left hand I ward off his left hand while stepping out straight ahead with my left foot. The knees should be bent as we sit into the posture, with the rear leg slightly extended. In this position, the left foot is full and the right foot empty. The points of the two hip bones should be level and facing forward. The *wei-lü* point at the base of the spine should be slightly drawn in so that we are perfectly erect. [This enables the spirit to reach the crown of the head. The front leg is 70 percent full and perpendicular to the ground. The rear leg has 30 percent active power and pushes forward.] At the same time as we step out with the left foot, the left hand gradually rises to a height level with the chest, palm facing in. The elbow hangs down slightly and our wrist lightly sticks to the opponent's arm somewhere between his wrist and elbow. Use the "spirit of emptiness" to control the opponent's arm and wait for his response. At the same time as the left hand rises, the right hand descends to the side of our right hip, hence the name of this posture.

Posture 4
Grasp Sparrow's Tail, Ward-off, Right

Continuing from the previous posture, if an opponent were to attack the left side of my chest and groin simultaneously with his right fist and left leg from my right side, then I would immediately position my right hand under the left in the attitude of holding a large ball (as in the earlier posture on the right side). I relax the left shoulder and protect the groin with the right arm. When the opponent realizes his power has landed on emptiness, he will react, and just then I quickly turn my right hip, rotate my heel to the left, and step out an inch or so. The knees should be bent as we sit into the posture. The right elbow immediately rises in the Ward-off motion at chest level, the palm of the hand facing in. The left hand plays a supporting role and is positioned between the right elbow and our chest. The eyes gaze straight ahead. The left leg should be extended and the toes of the left foot should have rotated slightly in with the turning of the waist in order to augment the Ward-off energy of the right elbow in contacting the opponent. This never fails to throw an opponent for a great distance.

Posture 5
Grasp Sparrow's Tail, Roll Back

Continuing from the previous posture, if the opponent neutralizes my Ward-off and applies Push against me, I immediately relax my right arm and circle it around the outside of his left elbow and over it. That is, with the inner side of my elbow, I stick to and follow my opponent's left elbow joint. At the same time, with the back of my left wrist, I stick to his left palm as he pushes me. Simultaneously, I quickly sit into my rear leg, turning the waist to the left. The backs of both elbows also follow the waist and rotate to the left, neutralizing my opponent's Push and making him lose his balance. At this moment it is possible to pull him, repel him, grasp him, or use Elbow-stroke. It is entirely up to me and there is plenty of latitude for choice. [There are two important points to remember in this movement. First, at all times the vision follows the movement of the head, remaining straight ahead and level. When the turning of the waist comes to a stop, the vision also comes to rest. Second, as the waist turns, the hands follow. When the waist is at rest, the movement of the hands also ceases. However, the extra energy which continues after the impetus of the movement

ceases is called "swing." Before the swing comes to a halt, it connects with the next movement. This is the key to T'ai-chi ch'üan. It is precisely that movement produces swing, which in turn connects again with movement. Movement and swing; swing and movement. There is no break between the two. If there is the slightest gap, a break will occur. I hope you will pay special attention to this as I will not repeat it again.]

Posture 6
Grasp Sparrow's Tail, Press

Continuing from the previous posture, if the opponent withdraws his arm, I turn over my right wrist and with the outside of my right elbow stick to the outside of his left arm. I support my right hand with the left, using the palm to follow and stick to the area between the right elbow and wrist. To take advantage of his withdrawing arm, I extend my left leg and let my weight rest on the right. Following the rotation of the waist, my line of vision gradually shifts to the fore as I press up and out. This will surely cause the opponent to spring out of his stance.

Posture 7
Grasp Sparrow's Tail, Push

Continuing from the previous posture, if the opponent neutralizes my Press and counters by raising his right arm to press me, I immediately turn my right wrist and push his right wrist joint with my palm. I separate my left hand and with the palm of that hand push his right elbow. At first I use lifting energy to lift it back, and then push straight ahead. The waist and legs work simultaneously along with the vision to send the opponent off. The opponent will surely be repelled by this action.

Posture 8
Single Whip

Continuing from the previous posture, if the opponent attacks me from the rear and to the left, I immediately shift my weight to the left leg, sit into it, and raising the toes of the right foot, rotate to the left and rear. Both left and right arms are extended at shoulder height and level in front of me. The elbows should be slightly sunk with the palms facing down. Together they follow the waist, turning all the way into the corner to our left and rear. The right foot also follows, rotating 120 degrees. Now bend the right leg and sit into it. At the same time the two hands follow this movement by swinging back. The right hand arrives at a point beside the right armpit with the five fingers close together and hanging like a hook. The left palm facing up seems to support it as it also draws back, stopping at a point below the right armpit and above the bottom of the ribs. Now begin to withdraw the heel of the left foot, while the knees and hips draw back at the same time. Simultaneously, the right arm and hook-hand extend in the direction of the right corner, as it were, "seeking the straight in the bent." At the same time lift the left leg and sit into it. The right leg also begins to straighten. At the same time, the left hand, palm facing in, rotates around at chest level with the movement of the waist to a point 180 degrees to the rear of the previous posture. As the toes of the right foot rotate into position following the waist and knee, the left palm turns over and is pressed against the opponent's chest. Sink the shoulders and drop the elbows. Seek the straight in the bent. The line of vision follows the movement as if to propel the opponent away. This never fails to throw the opponent for a great distance. This posture seeks to develop stability within extension. Although the arms and legs are extended and moving away from the body, the *ch'i* must maintain Central Equilibrium.

Posture 9
Raise Hands

Continuing from the previous posture, if the opponent once again attacks from the right side, then I immediately rotate my body to the right and sit into the left leg, lifting the right foot and moving it to the right front side, lightly touching the ground with the heel, the toes slightly raised. The knee is slightly bent. The left and right arms simultaneously open outward with the palms facing in towards each other and gradually moving closer together and upward. They should rise until the right palm and right leg are in a straight line facing forward, with the left palm in a supporting position beside the left ribs. The right hand is in front and the left behind, both hands in the same at-

titude. The backs of the wrists are extended and point forward with a slight arch. The idea is that when sticking to the opponent's wrists, one gathers energy and raises them in order to wait for a change in the situation. If one can raise them with energy and instantly release them, then without exception, the opponent will be thrown. This posture may also be adopted as a form of standing meditation. It is the stabilizing energy of raising and bringing together. Therefore, as we execute Advance, Retreat, Gaze-left, and Look-right, seizing and releasing are under our control and not our opponent's.

Posture 10
Shoulder-Stroke

Continuing from the previous posture, if the opponent quickly rises and attempts to attack me again, then I simultaneously withdraw my right arm, left hand, and right foot, causing my opponent's attacking energy to land on nothing. Then I step out with my right foot straight ahead and rest my weight on it. The right hand hangs downward protecting the groin, while the left hand plays a supporting role behind the right elbow. The right shoulder follows the energy of the waist and legs, as together with the line of vision, we press forward in a leaning attitude. The opponent is invariably toppled by this technique.

Posture 11
White Crane Cools Wings

Continuing from the previous posture, if the opponent assails me from the left side with feet and fists, then I immediately raise my right hand towards the left until it is in front of my face at the height of the temple, thus neutralizing the energy of his right fist which was attacking my head. The left hand separates in a downward direction to a level beside the hip, thus brushing aside the opponent's right foot which is aimed at my groin. At the same time, the left foot is raised and drawn in with the toes just touching the ground in order to protect the groin. In this way the opponent's posture is completely scattered and disorganized.

Posture 12
Brush Knee Twist Step, Left

Continuing from the preceding posture, if the opponent attacks my mid or lower section with fist or feet, I immediately sink my body, with the weight still on the right foot. The right hand turns over with the palm facing up and descends following the waist. When it reaches the right hip, then the left leg lifts and steps out, the heel making first contact with the ground. At the same time the left hand follows the right hand as far as the right hip in readiness for the brushing motion. Then the right arm rotates and rises upward from the rear. When it reaches ear level, the fingertips advance forward with the wrist horizontal as if seeking to pierce the opponent's chest. At the same time, the left hand brushes aside the opponent's fist or leg and arrives beside the left hip, with the palm of the hand facing down. Resting the weight on the left leg and relaxing the waist and hips, I sink the shoulders and drop the elbows. The right palm again follows the line of vision, and as the right leg straightens, pushes directly forward. The opponent is invariably thrown by this technique.

Posture 13
Play Guitar

From the preceding posture, if the opponent uses his left hand to block my right palm and his right hand to attack the right side of my chest, I immediately lift my right foot, and with the toes slightly turned out, rest all my weight on it to form the stance. The right palm rises and withdraws following the back of the opponent's right wrist and then seizes and presses down towards the left. At the same time the left hand rises, sticking to the opponent's right elbow, draws back and together in the manner of holding a guitar. Thus, the opponent's elbow and arm are in danger of being broken. In every way the opponent is under my control. This is called "Play Guitar."

Brush Knee Twist Step, Left

The explanation for this posture is the same as for Posture 12 and the basic idea is similar.

Postures 14 & 15
Step Up, Block, Parry, and Punch

Continuing from the preceding posture, if the opponent parries my right palm with his left hand and with his right fist attempts to attack my chest, I immediately withdraw, resting my weight on the rear leg, while the right palm descends to the left hip to protect the groin. Realizing that his attacking fist has landed on nothing, the opponent then attempts to deliver a kick to my groin. However, perceiving that the opponent is already at a disadvantage, I quickly turn the toes of the left foot three inches or so to the left and rest my weight on it. At the same time, I lift the right foot and take a half step to the right front and rest my weight on it. The right hand forms a fist, and following the waist, twists forward, moving from left to right and turning over until it reaches a point below the right ribs in order to neutralize the opponent's attacking fist. This is called "Block."

At the same time, the left hand, following the waist, moves to the rear and then again rises rotating to the level of the ear. The "standing palm" in the left hand continues thrusting straight ahead to defend against the opponent's attacking fist and causing it to land on nothing, while I withdraw my other arm in preparation for attack. This is called "Parry."

Just as the left hand is arriving, I lift the left foot and take a step forward. The heel touches the ground and the weight shifts forward. The right fist, following the waist and right leg, delivers the punch, attacking from under cover of the left palm and wrist. The opponent has no time to protect himself and success is assured 100 percent. The subtlety of this technique requires thorough practice and detailed scrutiny. Only then can it be mastered.

Posture 16
Apparent Close-up

As with the preceding posture, if the opponent tugs at my right elbow with his left hand and pulls my right wrist with his right hand, I relax my right fist and withdraw it from the direction of the left shoulder. Sitting back into the rear leg I escape and neutralize his pulling energy. The left palm turns over face up, sliding underneath the right elbow with the palm of the hand following the elbow and protecting the arm, thus slipping away from and neutralizing the tugging power of my opponent's left wrist. At the same time, the two arms form a diagonal cross, with the palms facing in and coming together in front of the breast, thus completely neutralizing the opponent's seizing energy. This is called "Sealing Up," just like sealing a door. At the same time I depress the chest and relax the waist and hips. My left hand lightly grasps and sticks to the opponent's left wrist, while my right hand sticks to his left elbow as I push forward shifting my weight to the left leg. This is called "Close up," like closing a gate. It is impossible to open. This technique turns disadvantage to advantage, and when executed in a relaxed manner, puts me in the controlling position with no effective opposition.

Posture 17
Cross Hands

Continuing from the preceding posture, if two opponents once again simultaneously attempt to strike down at me from the right side, I immediately elevate my right arm and following the waist and legs, open out towards the right. The left arm also turns with the waist and at the same time the toes of the left foot rotate inward to face straight ahead and reinforce the posture, thus throwing off attackers from both sides. If the opponents attempt to take advantage of my vulnerability by using two fists to attack my chest, then I turn my body and sit back into my left leg.

My two hands, following the movement, fall and then come together. My two wrists stick to the opponent's wrists and form a diagonal cross. This is "Cross Hands." At the same time, the right foot is lifted and draws back a step to face straight ahead as in the Preparation posture. This illustrates the principle that when opening reaches its peak there is once again closing, or the marvelous function of "one opening and one closing." However, although the two feet are parallel in Cross Hands, the left is full while the right is empty. It is not a "horse stance." The horse stance is double-weighted. This is strictly forbidden in T'ai-chi ch'üan. One must not fail to take note of this.

Posture 18
Embrace Tiger, Return To Mountain

Continuing from the preceding posture, if an opponent once again attacks from the right rear, with no opportunity to determine whether he is using fists or feet, then I quickly turn my waist and separate my two hands. The palm of my right hand faces down and the left palm up. The left hand falls to the left and rear, brushing aside the opponent as he attempts to make contact. Quickly lifting my right foot, I take a step to the right rear and shift my weight to it. As the right hand brushes the knee, the wrist rotates so that the palm faces up as if "embracing a tiger." This enables me to protect my groin and at the same time attempt to embrace the opponent's waist. If I should fail to embrace it securely, then I quickly rotate my left palm and attack his face. If I still have not hit the mark, the opponent will certainly withdraw his right hand and attack with his left. I then respond by using Roll-back to neutralize him and continue with the three postures of Grasp Sparrow's

Tail—Roll-back, Press, and Push—followed by Diagonal Single Whip. The explanation for these is the same as above. In T'ai-chi ch'üan sparring, every move is followed by three moves as a precaution. If one observes this at all times, one can certainly expect to be successful.

Diagonal Single Whip is executed in the direction of the left rear corner. See explanation for Single Whip.

Posture 19
Fist Under Elbow

Continuing from the preceding posture, if the opponent attacks me with his fist from the left side, I shift my weight backwards, causing his energy to land on nothing. Quickly lifting my left foot and moving it, sole level with the ground to face directly left, I take a step forward and

shift my weight to it, thus getting into position to meet the attack. At the same time, my left palm opens outward to pull the opponent's arm, while the right "hook-hand" relaxes open and follows the rotation of the waist in order to destabilize his offensive posture. Simultaneously the right leg moves towards the right front and takes a step with the toes facing right and parallel with the left heel. The full weight is then shifted to it. As the center of gravity rotates, the two arms follow the turning of the waist and expand outward to neutralize the opponent's offensive. When the right forward hand reaches a point facing the chest, and when the left hand is behind the armpit, lift the left foot and bring it forward, placing the heel down first. At the same time the left wrist, anticipating a capture by the opponent, describes a small circle and from beneath the armpit thrusts with straight fingers directly for the opponent's throat. The right hand, beginning in front of the chest, forms a fist and is drawn back in hiding beneath the left elbow. In the event that the left hand is captured by the opponent, the right hand can immediately strike straight for his stomach. This never fails to hit the mark and those hit invariably topple. Do not use it lightly and be extremely careful.

Posture 20
Repulse Monkey, Right

Continuing from the preceding posture, if the opponent grasps my left forearm with his right hand and with his left hand immobilizes the fist under my elbow, then unable to free myself, I endure his control for the moment and immediately relax my fist. With palm facing up, it is withdrawn to a point beside the right hip. The left wrist turns over, advances forward and presses down to neutralize his gripping power. If I have not yet escaped, I quickly withdraw my left leg and take a step directly backwards. The left hand and wrist turn over palm up in order to escape, withdrawing towards the left hip. The right palm rotates, moving towards the rear, until the fingertips are level with the ear. At this point I can directly stab for the opponent's throat or use the palm to strike his chest. At the same time the toes of the right foot rotate to face directly ahead to complete the posture. This movement transforms retreat into advance, defense into offense. Its effectiveness is completely dependent on the waist. Study it carefully.

In this movement, the two feet move backwards with each foot pointing straight ahead. This will not be understood by the casual practitioner. T'ai-chi ch'üan originated with the Taoists. If one has not yet succeeded in opening the "Three Gates" through meditation, then practicing Repulse Monkey is indispensable. If the toes of the two feet are even slightly turned out, the *wei-lü* gate will be locked. This secret can only be shared by those who understand.

Posture 21
Repulse Monkey, Left

The directions are the same for Repulse Monkey, Left and Right.

Posture 22
Diagonal Flying

Continuing from the preceding posture, if the opponent grasps my right wrist from the right side, I immediately turn over my wrist and bring it down towards my left hip. Simultaneously the left hand circles up and is held palm down below the armpit and in front of the chest in order to protect the right arm. If the opponent releases my right wrist and quickly grabs my left elbow and wrist, I immediately relax and sink my left arm, and raising my right arm beginning at the hip and left armpit, attack the right side of the opponent's neck and throat with the palm up in a "diagonal flying" motion. As a result the opponent is rendered helpless. At the same time the right leg steps out to the right rear corner and my weight is shifted to it in order to transmit the power of the right palm. The toes of the left foot follow the waist and rotate towards the right to augment the issuing energy. The left wrist sinks to an assisting position beside the left knee, thus completing the posture. If our palm finds its target, the opponent will surely be sent flying for a distance of several yards.

Posture 23
Cloud Hands

Continuing from the preceding posture, if the opponent raises his left arm, turns over my right palm, and with his right fist attacks the right side of my chest, I immediately turn over and relax my right wrist and draw it back to a point beside my right armpit. At the same time, the left hand, following the waist, rotates all the way to the right and comes to a stop besides the right hip, with the two hands in an embracing attitude. The left foot steps out directly to the left front, both to relax the waist and neutralize the attacking energy, and to prepare to protect the groin. If the opponent realizes that his attack has landed on nothing and quickly withdraws his fist to attack the left side of my chest, while simultaneously raising his right leg as if to attack my groin, then I relax the left side of my chest, sink my left hip, and rotate my waist all the way to the left, taking a half step laterally with the toes of my right foot pointing forward, and shift to it as in the Beginning posture. At the same time, I raise the left hand, palm facing in, and sticking to the opponent's hand, pass it in front of myself at throat level in order to neutralize the opponent's energy. The right palm descends and follows the left hand in rotating around to form an embracing attitude beside the left hip just as on the right side. Thus the opponent's leg which is aimed at my groin lands on nothing. With this posture the opponent uses hands and feet in a wild manner, but I respond with perfect ease as if completely relaxed. This is why this posture is called Cloud Hands. It means that we move as if we were in clouds or water. Truly this is an example of action resulting from non-action.

As the waist revolves, although it appears as if we were sitting in the middle, nevertheless we must still clearly distinguish full and empty. We must not be double-weighted. The rotation of the two hands follows the waist as they pass the center line. The top hand is just level with the throat, while the bottom hand faces the navel. The upper body is erect as in the Beginning posture. There should not be the slightest hint of leaning or discontinuity. The effectiveness of this posture is completely dependent upon the rotation of the waist and hips. Only in this way can we pull up the opponent's rooting power and topple him. Students must earnestly strive to grasp this.

Posture 24

Cloud Hands, Right, repetition of Cloud Hands, Left and Single Whip are the same as above.

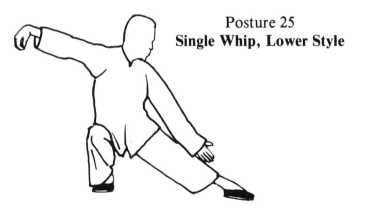

Posture 25
Single Whip, Lower Style

Continuing from the preceding posture, if the opponent grabs my left hand with his right, I immediately rotate the toes of my right foot to the right so that they are pointing directly forward, while shifting my weight to the rear.

The left foot rotates inward 25 degrees. At the same time the left hand withdraws to a point in front of the waist and hips. The fingertips travel downward following a line from the knee to the heel as they advance forward. [The waist, hips, and *wei-lü* sink downwards.] The left foot is still open at an angle of 50 degrees. The right "hook hand" continues to balance it, causing the opponent to totally lose his grasping power, and thus my posture is complete.

Posture 26
Golden Cock Stands on One Leg, Right

From the preceding posture, if the opponent comes to his own rescue with his left hand, attempting to pull my hand back with force, I then follow the force, gathering my body together and rising. With my right hand I aim for his larynx and with my right knee I attack his groin. The toes should hang relaxed. If the opponent withdraws to avoid the attack, I can immediately change and raise the toes to kick the groin. The left knee is slightly bent to stabilize the stance. The left palm should sink to a supporting position beside the left hip in order to balance the posture.

Posture 27
Golden Cock Stands on One Leg, Left

Refer to the explanation above for Golden Cock Stands on One Leg, Right.

Posture 28
Right Separation of the Foot

From the preceding posture, if the opponent attempts to make contact with my left hand, I immediately turn my wrist over facing up, and following the waist and legs to the left, relax and sink towards the left rear. I then raise the right palm, place it on the opponent's left elbow, and "roll back" with it. At the same time, the right foot becomes empty and there is a slight shift to the left front to augment

the power. At this point, the opponent realizes his power is lost, and will certainly attempt to retreat. I then rotate my left wrist and stealthily use Pull-down force to coordinate with the Roll-back, placing it on top of the right wrist to form a diagonal "Cross Hands." If the opponent withdraws his hand and attacks again, then I separate my right hand, grasp the opponent's left wrist and quickly raise my right foot to kick the opponent's left knee, shin, or the right side of his ribs. The toes and back of the foot should be level and in a straight line. [The knee should be raised so that it and the leg are horizontal.] The line of vision should follow the direction of the right hand and be concentrated. The left hand, in the "standing palm" position, opens level with the right hand to balance it. [The two arms open to the left and right until they reach a point level with the shoulders. The right hand and the right foot should form one straight line and the left hand and left foot should also form a straight line....The right foot is drawn back, and without touching the ground, is then directed to the right front side where it is placed down. Bend the knee and rest the weight on it. At the same time the right hand, following the waist and hips, withdraws with the palm turned up to a point beneath the left elbow in a Roll-back motion to the right....The right arm drops to the right rear and rises, describing a large circle, until it reaches a point between the shoulder and right ear. The left arm descends to the side of the right hip. The feet have not yet moved. At this point the right hand descends and the left hand rises to meet it, forming an intersection with the two wrists. The left foot then rises slightly and takes half a step forward....Now the two wrists rotate outward while the feet remain stationary.]

Posture 29
Left Separation of the Foot

The same explanation applies as above. Left and right switch. You may refer to this yourselves.

Posture 30
Turn Body, Kick With Heel

Continuing from the preceding posture, if an opponent attacks with his right hand from the left rear side, I immediately bring my left hand and left foot back to my center and slightly raise the toes of my right foot. At the same time, the right hand makes a slight waving motion as it follows the waist and hips in rotating to the left rear. After the right wrist rotates around, it joins the left wrist on top and then separates to the rear side. The left hand grasps the opponent's right wrist while the right hand opens to the right rear with a "standing palm" to balance the left hand. The left heel kicks in the direction of the opponent's groin. The right knee is slightly bent, giving stability to the power of the heel. The vision is directed in a straight line with the fingertips of the left hand. The opponent will certainly be toppled by our kick.

Left and Right Brush Knee
These are the same as described above.

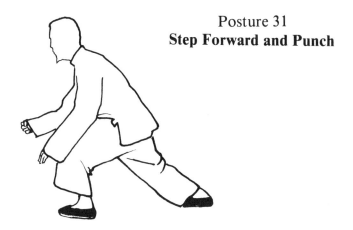

Posture 31
Step Forward and Punch

From the preceding posture, if the opponent attempts to kick with his left leg, I immediately relax my waist, sit back and turn out the toes of my right foot. Simultaneously, I turn over my right hand and form a fist with it, knuckles up, beside my right hip. The left hand is also brought over beside the right hip. My center of gravity is shifted to the right leg as I take a long step with the left. My weight is then shifted to it. Synchronously with this shift, the left hand brushes to the left. As the opponent falls to his right, I attack the left side of his waist with my right fist. This is Punch.

Step Up To Ward-Off

Continuing from the preceding posture, if the oppnent turns around and attacks again with his left hand, I immediately sit back into my rear leg, turn out the toes of the left foot and shift the weight to it. The right hand fist relaxes open and moves up in the Ward-off attitude. The right leg follows the movement and takes a forward step. The remaining movements—Roll-back, Press, Push and Single Whip—are the same as above. Refer to the previous explanation.

Posture 32
Fair Lady Works Shuttles

Continuing from the preceding posture, if an opponent to our rear and right attacks with his right hand in a downward motion, I sit back into my rear leg, rotate the toes of my front foot as far to the right as possible and shift the weight to it. I then rotate the left palm up and draw it back beneath the right armpit. The right heel is drawn in and a half step is taken slightly to the right front. I then shift the weight to it. The left leg takes a step out in the direction of the right rear corner and the weight is shifted to it. The left palm follows the right elbow and wrist as they move up and turn out with the palms facing out and sticking to the opponent's right hand. The right palm then passes the left elbow, pushing towards the right side of the opponent's ribs. The right knee should be slightly extended to project the power. This never fails to throw an opponent. This posture can be used to attack the left and right, suddenly hiding and suddenly appearing. We remain elusive while looking for opportunities to attack an opening. Therefore, we call this posture "Fair Lady Works Shuttles" to symbolize its skill and effectiveness.

Posture 33
Fair Lady Works Shuttles, II

Continuing from the preceding posture, to respond to an opponent coming from our rear and right, the method is the same as described above. Only the direction of our turn is different. First, I shift my weight and sit back into the rear leg. The toes of the left foot follow the waist, turning as far as possible to the right. The right palm is turned up beneath the left armpit, while the body rotates 180 degrees and takes a step towards the 270 degree corner to our right. Bend the leg and sit into it. The rest is the same as above.

Fair Lady Works Shuttles, III

Continuing from the preceding posture, shift the weight to the rear leg. Turn the left palm up and place it beneath the right elbow as mentioned above. Take a step at a 90 degree angle towards the corner. The rest is the same as above.

Fair Lady Works Shuttles, IV

Continuing from the preceding posture, rotate 270 degrees to the right hand corner and take a step. The rest is the same as for Fair Lady, II.

Grasp Sparrow's Tail (Ward-off, Roll-back, Press, and Push) and Single Whip Lower Style are all the same as above.

Posture 34
Step Up To Seven Stars

Continuing from the preceding posture (which is used to defend against an opponent slicing down with his right hand) after his power has landed on nothing, I raise my body with the weight on the left leg, while the right leg advances a half step, but remains empty, with the toes just touching the ground. The right "hook-hand" relaxes open and falls, moving forward simultaneously with the right leg to a point in front of the chest and forming a fist at the same

time as the left hand. The two wrists intersect and support each other as they attack the opponent's solar plexus. This blow is extremely devastating. Its victims are unlikely to escape serious danger. Those who use it should not do so lightly.

Posture 35
Retreat To Ride Tiger

Continuing from the preceding posture, if the opponent uses his two hands in a hooking and hanging motion to separate my two fists and advances his right leg to attack my groin, I quickly withdraw my right leg and shift my weight to it. The left leg is raised and takes a half step back, remaining empty with the toes just touching the ground. I then withdraw the right fist, and circling around to the right rear, bring it up in the "standing palm" position at the ready beside the right shoulder to attack the *T'ai-yang* point

at the opponent's right temple. The left fist descends and opens, brushing the left knee in order to brush aside the opponent's leg and protect my groin. In describing this posture we say that, although the opponent's attack is as fierce as a tiger, we are able to mount and ride it.

Posture 36
Turn Body Sweep Lotus Leg

Continuing from the preceding posture, if an opponent attacks from the rear, putting me in the position of being attacked simultaneously from the front and back, I immediately relax my right "standing palm" and circle it to a position between my waist and ribs to gather energy. The left arm opens out towards the left to assist in "turning the rudder" and rotating the body. The left foot lifts slightly and the toes of the right foot stand up. At the same time, lift the left leg and first move it slightly to the left and then to the right in order to propel the whole body in a 360 degree circle. [The right heel must not shake even slightly. Pay serious attention to this. Turn until the left foot touches the ground facing forward at a 45 degree angle with the toes lightly touching the ground. The two arms swing around until level with the chest, palms facing down.] By using the left hand and left foot together a hurricane force is created high and low against the opponent to the rear in a fanning attack at his cheeks and knees. The left foot then touches down, and the weight is shifted to it. The toes of the right foot touch the ground without weight. At this point, the opponent in front of us will attempt to attack, but I stick to his left elbow and wrist with my two hands. Once again I raise my right leg, and in a motion from left to right, use horizontal force to sweep the left side of his waist just like a strong wind shaking the leaves of the lotus plant. [Making a clockwise circle in front of my groin, the toes lightly touch the fingertips of both hands.] Without relaxing and sinking the waist and hips, the effectiveness of this movement will not be realized. However, this technique is vicious and

should not be used indiscriminately. Be very careful! [There are two points to pay attention to in this movement. First, the two hands must not shake. Second, if you are not able to raise the right foot very high and touch the fingertips, do not strain. After long practice it will come naturally, so you should not worry.]

Posture 37
Bend Bow Shoot Tiger

Continuing from the preceding posture, if the opponent returns the attack using "Apparent Close Up," for example, then I withdraw my right leg and touch down to the right front. The two hands follow the waist and hips, circling towards the right rear. When the right hand reaches a point level with the right ear, the two hands both form fists. The left fist sinks beside the left hip to strike the opponent's stomach. The right fist arrives even with the right side of the forehead to strike sideways at the opponent's left *T'ai-yang* point. The "tiger's mouths" of the two fists face each other as if "bending a bow to shoot a tiger." This is a boastful way of referring to the posture, which is sufficient to repel the fiercest opponent.

Step Forward Block, Parry, and Punch, Apparent Close Up and Cross Hands are all the same as above.

Closing the T'ai-chi Form

Continuing from the preceding posture, if the opponent attacks my two wrists with his two fists using great force to press down, I relax and open my two hands and allow then to fall to the sides of my hips. The two legs follow the downward movement of the two hands and straighten to a standing position as in the Beginning posture. As a result, the opponent's pressure lands on nothing and he will certainly be thrown for a fall and go down on his knees before me. As this movement ends the whole form, students must no forget that "Closing the T'ai-chi Form" means uniting *yin* and *yang*, the four duograms, eight trigrams and sixty-four hexagrams and making them once again revert to T'ai-chi [the Great Ultimate]. This also means gathering in the mind and the breath and allowing them both to revert to the *tan-t'ien*. Concentrate the spirit and calm all cares. Doing just the right amount and no more, we will not become scattered and will never make a laughing stock of ourselves before experts.

XVII. Push-Hands

From
Thirteen Chapters

Grasp Sparrow's Tail, explained and illustrated above, embodies the basic movements for Push-hands. Moreover, in Chapter 11, which explains the stages of progress, what we called the "stage of Heaven," or the three levels of conscious movement—listening to energy, interpreting energy, and perfect clarity—are all grounded in Push-hands. We must advance in progressive stages from listening to energy to the level of perfect clarity. This indeed is the ultimate! Students should begin with Push-hands and practice until they are thoroughly familiar with it. Only then can they accomplish anything. The following photographs illustrate the style of Push-hands characterized by Ward-off, Rollback, Press, and Push, the four sides of the square, forgetting oneself and following others, stick, join, adhere and follow, and fixed foot position. Ward-off (*peng*), Rollback (*lü*), Press (*chi*), and Push (*an*) are special jargon used by martial artists and do not exactly correspond with dictionary definitions of these words, so do not confuse them. We have already explained in detail above and will not repeat this again. The photographs are of myself and K'uo Sheng-ch'in, referred to in the text for the convenience of readers as A and B respectively, A being myself. All succeeding photographs follow this format.

Part 1: Ward-off

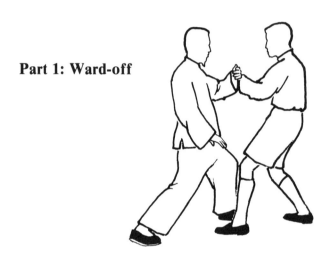

A extends his left hand in front of him in an embracing attitude and sticks to the area between B's left elbow and wrist. He sits with his weight on the left leg in the posture Ward-off. The right hand opens out beside the right hip to balance it. B's hands and feet should be exactly the same as A's. The movement and key points to remember will be explained under the corresponding photographs. This is also called "One Hand Push-Hands." One Hand Push-Hands is the beginning of the study of Push-hands and the first step in practicing relaxation of the hands and arms. It is simply the use of left and right, backwards and forwards, up and down in mutual give and take in order to test our ability to stick, join, adhere, and follow.

A's right elbow advances to the right front in an embracing attitude and sticks to B's right elbow with the palms facing in. The left hand plays a supporting role between the chest and elbow, palm facing out. The weight is on the right leg in the posture Ward-off, Right. The idea of Ward-off has already been described in detail in the chapter containing Yang's oral transmissions. To sum up, it is a great error to use force in warding off an opponent. Instead, one must use sticking energy to fasten to B's energy, sense his incoming Ward-off, and turn the waist to neutralize and cause it to land on nothing. Then, with four ounces of energy, it is possible to deflect and repel him, or even uproot him. The rest is the same.

Part 2: Press

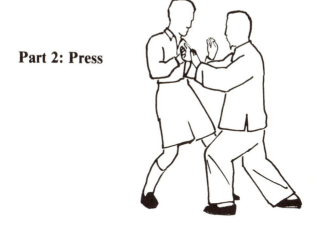

After A has executed Ward-off, Right and B has attempted to use sticking energy to raise it, then A's left palm joins the right arm between the elbow and wrist, while the body weight sits on the right leg. At the same time, the waist and hips push forward to assist the energy of Press in pressing forward. This technique of Press is used after we realize that B is attempting to stick to and elevate our Ward-off. If B has already used neutralizing energy, then A's Press will either immediately be absorbed or thrown off to the side. If B does not understand how to neutralize, but instead resists with force, then A must anticipate this by first applying sticking energy to raise him and follow this up by continuing to use pressing energy. B will then certainly be thrown for several yards.

Part 3: Roll-Back

After A's Press has been neutralized by B, then A immediately rotates his waist to the right and relaxes and sinks his right elbow in a downward direction. The right wrist again follows B's left elbow, and sticking, circles upward. In this way, A's right elbow will stick precisely to B's left elbow. At the same time, the back of the left wrist sticks to B's left pushing hand, and the weight is shifted to the rear leg. The right elbow and left wrist simultaneously turn slightly up in order to neutralize B's pushing energy in the direction of the left rear corner and cause it to land on nothing. In this way the technique is successful. This energy is the most difficult to apply in Push-hands. If there is the slightest error in the technique, then B's energy will be rolled back on our own body. We will be unable to neutralize it, and instead will be thrown by B's Push and Press. Therefore, this technique is tantamount to "opening the gates to greet bandits." Its usefulness consists in luring the opponent into deep penetration of our territory and causing him to fall into our trap where we can then capture him. The essence of this technique lies in there being intention and no intention, not slipping and not sticking, and making our move if an opportunity arises. Its usefulness is unlimited.

Part 4: Push

When A uses Roll-back energy to roll back, B stores his energy and does not dare to press forward. A then takes his right palm and pushes against the back of the wrist of

B's right hand and with the left palm pushes aganst B's right elbow. The vision should be straight and level. The waist and hips follow the forward leg in advancing so as to augment the pushing power. Without exception B will be thrown for a fall. If this technique is not successful, there are three possible changes. One, if A misses the right opportunity, then the energy of Push will be neutralized by B and will very likely land on nothing. Two, if A does not maintain the power advantage, but clashes with B's energy, then he will lose control of the situation. Third, if A fails both to seize the proper opportunity and to maintain the power advantage, and is also unclear in listening to energy and dares to use strength in pushing, then he will certainly be thrown for a great distance. Students should be very aware of this and only then will they be successful.

XVIII.
Ta-Lü

From
Thirteen Chapters

Ta-lü is four corners Push-hands. It makes use of the four methods: Pull-down, Split, Elbow-stroke, and Shoulder-stroke, which correspond to the four trigrams: *Chen, Hsün, Ken*, and *Tui*. These are used to supplement Ward-off, Roll-back, Press, and Push of Four Sides Push-Hands, which correspond to the trigrams: *Ch'ien, K'un, K'an,* and *Li*. This accords with the *I ching*'s principle that, "*Yin* and *yang* exchange and the eight hexagrams succeed each other." T'ai-chi never departs from *yin* and *yang*, the eight trigrams, and the Five Elements. The Five Elements are used mainly in *San-Shou*. They are not included here, but will be discussed in detail later. Pull-down, Split, Elbow-stroke and Shoulder-stroke are also specialized jargon, and just as with Ward-off, Roll-back, Press and Push, must be redefined without reference to other meanings.

Pull-down uses the thumb and middle finger to lightly grasp the opponent's wrist and to throw him by following his power position. For example, the Pull-down concealed in the posture Brush Knee is what we mean by Pull-down.

Split is used when the opponent pushes tightly against our elbow. I follow the balance of power and neutralize the opponent by withdrawing my hand and counter-attacking his head as in the postures Stork Cools Wings and Ride Tiger. This is what is meant by Split. Elbow-stroke means using the elbow joint to attack an opponent, as in the Elbow-strokes concealed in the postures Step Up, Parry and Punch, and Hook-hand. These are examples of Elbow-stroke. Shoulder-stroke makes use of the shoulder to follow the power situation and attack an opponent, as in the Shoulder-stroke that follows Raise Hands. This is what we mean by Shoulder-stroke. The following photographs are of myself and senior fellow student Li Shou-chien. Once again we use A and B as with the Push-hands photographs. I am designated as A. Instructions for the method are as follows.

Part 1: Making Contact

To make the initial contact, A and B stand facing each other. The orientation east or west, north or south makes no difference. Each one extends his right arm in the Ward-off position and shifts all the weight to the left leg while emptying and slightly elevating the right foot. Apply the left palm to the right arm in an "empty" Press position.

Part 2: Pull-down

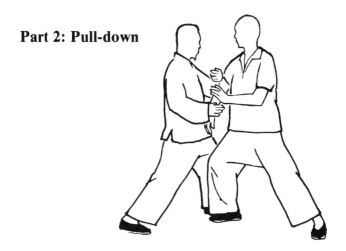

B sits into his right leg, while the left foot takes a step towards the left front. He then advances his right leg, stepping into A's groin area while attacking A's chest and rib region with a Shoulder-stroke. A then withdraws one step with his right leg in the direction of the right rear corner, while using his left elbow to roll back B's right elbow. With his right hand he pulls down B's right wrist. This is Pull-down.

Part 3: Split

After A has pulled down B's wrist, but has been neutralized, A then withdraws his right hand and circles around to the right rear and thrusts at B's face. This is what is meant by Split.

Part 4: Shoulder-stroke

After A uses Split, B wards off with his right arm and withdraws his right foot until it is even with his left. The heel of the left foot then turns out to the left 45 degrees, and the weight is shifted to it. The right foot again withdraws, taking a step into the right rear corner, still in the posture Roll-back and using Pull-down on A's right wrist. At the same time, A follows B's Pull-down power and brings his right leg back even with his left foot and rests his weight on it. He then takes a step to the left front with the left foot and immediately follows this up by stepping with the right leg into B's groin area and applying Elbow-stroke. This is Shoulder-stroke.

Part 5: Elbow-stroke

After B has neutralized A's Elbow-stroke by using the technique Split, A then advances his right arm in the Ward-off position, secretly concealing the elbow. One must act precisely at the moment when the opponent is about to withdraw but has not yet withdrawn. The usefulness of this technique is unlimited. This is Elbow-stroke.

XIX.
San-Shou

From
Thirteen Chapters

San-shou is free hand sparring with no fixed techniques. Push-hands and *Ta-lü* are for training one's skills. Training means learning to listen to energy and from listening to energy gradually awakening to interpreting energy. After one can interpret energy, then there is no such thing as training or not training, free or not free, sticking or not sticking, following or not following, and all this becomes irrelevant. The techniques for *San-shou* can be found in the Five Elements, or what we call Advance, Retreat, Gaze-left, Look-right, and Central Equilibrium. If one is able to interpret energy and master the techniques, one's applications will be successful. I studied with Master Yang Ch'eng-fu for seven years. I suffered much in my pursuit of this and it was very difficult to acquire.

There is a certain kind of energy called "receiving energy." If one can receive energy, this is the highest achievement in interpreting energy. When one's skill has been refined to this level, then it is useless even discussing other energies. Receiving energy is similar to being attacked by an opponent with a ball. If I just slightly resist or intercept it, it will bounce off. This is "bumping" energy and not receiving energy. A ball is light and thus is easily bounced back, but if we consider a ball of several hundred pounds, can it be bounced off with a single bump? Therefore, the use of bumping is not appropriate. Instead, we must seem to attract the incoming ball and then throw it out. This is receiving energy. If one can apply this method, whether slow or fast, light or heavy, then sticking, listening, and uprooting will all come naturally. Uniting, swallowing [absorbing], and spitting [issuing] are all performed in the wink of an eye. This energy operates in fractions of an inch and approaches the miraculous. What else can we say about *San-shou*? Therefore, I say that T'ai-chi's superiority derives precisely from this receiving energy.

PART THREE

XX. Selections on Meditation

From
Chung-yang jih-pao
(Central Daily News)

Meditation and Health

Chung-yang jih-pao (Central Daily News),
June 10, 1968

Longevity is a common aspiration of all mankind. The pursuit of long life requires the health of body and mind. If we desire health, in addition to nutrition, medicine, hygiene, and exercise, we must emphasize peace of mind.

In this complex society, we constantly experience confusion and tension, with no means to relax. Beset by worries, tension, restrictions and demands on all sides, the cerebrum is forced to work the entire day. Even in sleep we dream, so there is never a moment's rest. If we can temporarily forget our worries and tensions, thus enabling the body and mind to enjoy relaxation and happiness for a period and allowing the nerves an opportunity for true rest, this not only improves the health of body and mind, but can contribute to longevity and reverse the aging process.

What we mean by temporarily forgetting all cares and tensions is simply seizing a few moments of peace in the midst of this confused and stressful environmnt. The method for seizing these few moments of peace is meditation.

In my youth I was afflicted with rheumatism, and whenever the weather changed, I suffered unbearably. At least two or three times every year, I was forced to stay in bed for a week at a time. I sought treatment from both Chinese and Western doctors, including acupuncture and injections, but these only alleviated the symptoms for a short time, and then they would reappear. Later I received instruction in meditation from a friend who also introduced me to a number of ancient and contemporary works on internal cultivation. After practicing for one month I felt a warming of the *ch'i* in the *tan-t'ien*. Within two months this warmth gradually rose up my spine to waist level, and at three months my whole body perspired. Later on, the warm *ch'i* ascended along the spine to the shoulders and finally to the crown of the head. It is now five years that I have maintained this practice consistently for at least one half hour each day. Although I cannot claim that all my meridians are completely open, my rheumatism has never reappeared. At the same time my backaches and weak stomach were also rapidly cured. This must be the result of meditation.

Meditation is mental concentration. Everything is put aside in order to maintain the peace and tranquility of the mind and to strengthen the control function of the central nervous system. Moreover, deep breathing during meditation improves blood circulation, increases the absorbtion of nutrients, and promotes all metabolic processes.

According to biological research, within the human body, nutrients carried by the blood stream must be combined with oxygen provided by breathing in order for oxidation to occur. The carbon dioxide produced by oxidation must then be eliminated by the body in order to maintain the proper metabolic balance. Thus breath is even more important to us than food. When air enters the alveoli in the lungs, because the concentration of oxygen is higher in the air than in the air sacs and in accord with the law of osmosis, it penetrates the walls of the air sacs and enters the blood. Once in the blood stream, it is taken up by the hemoglobin in the red blood cells which then becomes oxygenated hemoglobin. These oxygen carrying red blood cells pass through the capillaries of the lungs and are distributed to every part of the body where they produce heat and energy. From this we can understand the great importance of breath to human health.

The average person takes approximately one very shallow breath every four or five seconds. The fresh air that is inhaled does not really deeply penetrate the air sacs, nor is the stale air fully expelled. Therefore, the process of making oxygen available and of eliminating carbon dioxide from the veins is never fully optimized. This has a great influence on the health of body and mind.

The method of breathing used during meditation is abdominal breathing. As we inhale the air, the lungs expand and fill to capacity, allowing it to deeply penetrate the air sacs and to maximize its distribution. At this moment the diaphragm is pushed downward, causing the belly to protude. When we exhale, the belly contracts, pushing upward, and completely expelling the stale air in the lungs. In this way, the exchange of gases in the lungs realizes its greatest efficiency. At the same time it constitutes a kind of exercise for the internal organs.

Although deep breathing during exercise also enhances the exchange of gases, it is seldom longer than ten minutes, while the meditator may often spend ten minutes, half an hour, or even several hours at a sitting. Also, with experience, one not only uses deep breathing during meditation, but at ordinary times one's breathing becomes deeper, longer, finer, and more even.

Most people are aware that exercise promotes blood circulation, improves the absorption of nutrients, and aids the process of metabolism. However, following exercise most people feel tired. We often see athletes lying on the grass after exercising with their eyes closed resting. This is an example of taking a moment of peace.

Many people are not fond of exercise. Also many people, because of circumstances in their life or work, do not have time or a suitable place for exercise. This is especially true for middle aged city dwellers over forty who, because of official responsibilities or business concerns, spend every day writing at their desks with no opportunity during the entire year to exercise. If they would meditate every day once or twice at a suitable time, it would be greatly beneficial to their mental and physical health.

Meditation certainly does not waste a lot of time. If every evening just before going to sleep or in the morning just after rising, we would simply meditate for twenty or thirty minutes on our beds, it will not interfere with our work schedule. Although these twenty or thirty minutes would seem to reduce our sleep time, in reality, they are even more beneficial than sleep. This is because during sleep our minds are scattered and sometimes we dream. However, meditation concentrates the mind, random thoughts are eliminated, and one enjoys tranquility and peace. This provides true rest for body and mind. Only from actual experience can one begin to understand this.

Meditation requires absolutely no special equipment or space. You can meditate in your own bedroom if the air is not too stale and it is not too noisy. If there are a number of children in the household, one can first put them to bed before meditating. If one has a choice of environments, then, of course, a place with a great expanse of ocean, or wide open skies, or all alone in an isolated country village would be best of all.

Postures and Methods of Meditation

Lightly close the mouth;
The eyelids hang like curtains.
Using abdominal breathing,
Eliminate all random thoughts.

The following is a detailed explanation of methods and postures for meditation:

1. Chair sitting. The body should be erect with face forward. The nose and navel and the ears and shoulders should be in alignment. The chin is slightly drawn in and the shoulders level. The waist should be straight and our seat stable. The spine should not be stretched too straight, but neither should it be bent. Relax all the muscles of the body without using any strength and be relaxed and natural.

2. Cross-legged sitting. Both legs are bent and the right foot is placed underneath the left thigh. The left foot is placed on the right thigh. This is the half-lotus posture. The full-lotus used by monks is even better. Another posture is the simple-seat, with legs crossed and feet under knees. In general, choose the most comfortable.

3. Hand position. The two hands, hanging naturally, are placed with the palms up on top of the legs. The palms are placed on top of each other with the tips of the thumbs touching and the "tiger's mouth" facing forward as if holding an object. The hands rest lightly in front of the stomach on top of the calves without pressure and naturally relaxed.

4. Reclining. Lying with the face up (too soft an inner spring mattress is not suitable), the back should be level and straight. The feet are extended level, with the toes pointing upward and naturally relaxed. The palms should face inward, lightly touching the sides of the thighs. The height of the pillow can be adjusted for comfort. All the muscles of the body should be relaxed. The eyes gaze in the direction of the abdomen.

5. First open the mouth and exhale the stale air from the lungs. Then close the mouth slowly and draw fresh air in through the nose. Repeat this 3 to 5 times in order to harmonize the breath.

6. Lightly close the mouth. The upper and lower lips and teeth should slightly touch. The tongue sticks to the hard palate.

7. The eyelids should hang like curtains. The vision extends from the bridge of the nose to the abdomen, but it is not necessary to concentrate. Our attitude should be one of gazing but not gazing, relaxed and natural. The eyes must not be completely shut in order to prevent falling asleep, and the light should not be too bright.

8. Abdominal breathing. Use deep breathing to allow air to completely fill the lungs, but do not expand the chest. The lung cavity expands downward from the pressure of the diaphragm. The downward movement of the diaphragm causes the abdomen to protrude slightly. When one exhales, the abdomen withdraws as the diaphragm is pressed upwards, forcing the stale air in the lungs to be completely expelled. The breathing should be deep, long, fine, even, light, and slow. There should be no sound.

    In the beginning, one must not force the breath to be deep and long. If normally one cycle of inhalation and exhalation takes four seconds, then during meditation it should be increased slightly to six seconds. After several days, this should be increased to eight seconds and gradually to ten. With long practice it can be increased to two or even one cycle per minute. The most advanced practitioners can breathe once in half an hour. In summary, beginners must not use force to hold the breath in order to avoid a feeling of oppression or discomfort. In slightly extending the length of exhalation, it should not be forced, but perfectly comfortable.

9. Eliminate random thoughts. All random thoughts must be completely banished. In the beginning, the mind is uncontrollable, and it is very difficult to achieve stillness. Simply suspend cogitation and sink the mind to the abdomen. At the same time, one should use the technique of counting the breaths. This causes the mind to focus on the count, and with practice random thoughts disappear.

10. Counting the breath. One inhalation and one exhalation is called a "breath." One breath equals one count. If you count the exhale, do not count the inhale, and vice versa. Count from one to ten or to one hundred. In the beginning, because random thoughts have not yet been eliminated, one often forgets the count in the middle. Simply start over from one. After a long time proficiency comes, and advanced practitioners can achieve stillness without counting at all.

11. Concentrate the mind. During meditation, the mind should be fixed on one point. In the beginning, one can focus on the *tan-t'ien* (a point in the lower abdomen). As one inhales, the mind should concentrate on the lower abdomen and imagine the air penetrating all the way to the abdomen. (In reality, the air only reaches the lungs, but even though it is impossible for it to reach the abdomen, one should imagine this.) When exhaling, also imagine that the air is exhaled from the abdomen. At an advanced level one can focus on other points, such as the *ni-wan* [crown of the head], *t'ien-t'ing* [middle of the forehead], *ming-t'ang* ["third eye" in the lower forehead], *shan-ken* [bridge of the nose], *chun-t'ou* [area under the nose] or *yung-ch'än* [ball of the foot], etc.

12. When finished meditating, open the mouth and expel three to five breaths to dissipate the heat of the body. Slowly rouse the body, gently stretching out the arms and legs. Rub the hands together to produce heat and massage the face, neck, shoulders, arms and legs while slowly standing up. Beginners, when they feel their legs becoming numb, should massage them until comfortable again. Under no circumstances stand up abruptly.

The preceding points are an elementary presentation of the fundamental methods and postures. More advanced practices will not be described at this time.

Meditation Corresponds Perfectly with Medical Principles; It Is the Bridge to Better Health and the Path to Longer Life

Chung-yang jih-pao (Central Daily News), June 10, 1968

During meditation the flow of saliva is greater than at ordinary times; it should be swallowed after we exhale and absolutely not expectorated. This is what Chinese books on internal cultivation refer to as "swallowing the saliva," and it is extremely beneficial. Although some modern scientists oppose swallowing saliva, Japanese physicians who have studied it for several decades have recently discovered that saliva contains a kind of nutritive element. One should not meditate immediately after eating, but wait an hour or two until the stomach is empty.

Perseverance Is Necessary in Meditation

Proficiency at meditation can increase blood circulation and raise the body temperature. This is a natural phenomenon. After long practice there will be warm *ch'i* in the *tan-t'ien* region. (This sensation may occur after several months or even several years.) After a time the warm *ch'i* may reach the waist and gradually ascend to the back and head regions. This sensation is extraordinarily pleasurable. Adepts have many different kinds of sensations, such as movement, itching, chills, warmth, lightness, heaviness, roughness, or smoothness, etc. These are the so called "Eight Sensations."

Perseverance is necessary for meditation, and one should practice at least once a day for more than fifteen minutes. One time in the morning and one in the evening is preferable. It is critically important to avoid lapses in practice. To run hot one day and cold for ten is without any benefit, while running hot for ten days and cold for one is also less than desirable.

Beginners at meditation should sit for short periods but frequently. This is because if they sit for a long time, they may become impatient and grow to dislike meditation. In the beginning one can meditate for five or ten minutes and then gradually extend the periods. Meditation must be approached with patience, and one cannot expect results overnight.

Afterword

Meditation is a form of inner cultivation and is considered a legitimate practice in every school of inner cultivation.

The meditation methods of the contemporary, Yin Shih Tzu, combine various forms of Buddhist and Taoist inner cultivation into one system.

Internal cultivation refers to our ancient Taoist practices of inner alchemy (*lien tan*), cultural movements (*tao-*

yin), and breathing exercises (*t'u-na*), together with Buddhist contemplation and meditation. Today teachers are divided into many different schools, some referring to "internal cultivation" (*nei-kung*) and some to "*ch'i* cultivation" (*ch'i-kung*), but all are methods of self-development. Although in movements, postures, and methods, each has its own specialty and tradition, in the end they all seek to strengthen the mind and train the body in order to attain longevity.

Our ancient methods of internal cultivation were transmitted to Japan where, after several decades of research, adaptation, and commentary, the Okada Meditation System was developed.

Our ancient books on internal cultivation are fond of using secret jargon and allusive language, causing readers to be lost in a fog and even suspect that it is superstitious, supernatural, secret, and strange. By writing in this arcane and esoteric style, it was impossible to fathom even a fraction of it without years of single-minded study and the instructions of an enlightened teacher.

Some say that meditation was a method of self-cultivation used by the Taoists and Buddhists and has nothing to do with our own generation. However, I must say that meditation, after investigation by modern specialists, has been found to be compatible with medicine and physiology and is truly the bridge to good health and the path to long life.

Meditation Has Three Secrets for Harmonizing Body and Mind

Meditation completely harmonizes the body,
    breath and mind.
Sitting with legs crossed harmonizes the body.
Calmness harmonizes the breath.
Controlling one's thoughts
    harmonizes the mind.

First, harmonize the body:
Before meditation, loosen the clothing and undo the belt. Take your seat in an easy and natural way. The body should be erect and the seat stable. The spine should not be stiffly straight nor should it be bent. The shoulders should be level, the waist extended, and all the muscles of the body relaxed. Now cross the legs, place the two hands one upon the other and rest them on top of the legs. Shake the body a few times from left to right in order to allow each part to be relaxed and natural.

Second, harmonize the breath:
Before meditating, open the mouth and expel a few breaths of stale air from the abdomen. The tongue lightly sticks to the hard palate with the lips and teeth lightly touching. Slowly inhale through the nostrils while imagining that each breath reaches all the way to the abdomen. Then once again exhale from the abdomen, and one will naturally achieve a state of calmness.

Third, harmonize the mind:
Most people's thoughts are random and confused. Early on in learning to meditate, people experience an increase in random thoughts as they enter a state of stillness. The more one thinks the further afield one's thoughts run. The mind is like a monkey, and one's thoughts like horses. It is most difficult to control. One must become indifferent to fame and fortune and put everything aside. The mind should focus on the abdomen, and the two eyes, slightly withdrawn, gaze down from the bridge of the nose to the abdomen. At the same time, use the technique of breath counting, and gradually one will be able to avoid confused thinking and eliminate all random thoughts.

Inscription for Foetal Breathing

Of the thirty-six swallows,
Number one comes first.
Our exhale should be very fine,
And our inhale slow and continuous.
Sitting or reclining are the same;
Be at ease walking or standing.
Beware of the impure,
And banish the foul.
Although we call it the "foetal breath,"
In reality it is the inner elixir.
Not only does it cure infirmities
And lengthen one's years,
But if practiced for a long time,
One's name may be added to the
List of Immortals.

XXI. Selection on the *I Ching*

From
I ch'üan
(The complete
I ching), Taipei:
Mei Ya Publications, 1976.

AUTHOR'S PREFACE TO
THE COMPLETE I CHING

I had read the *I ching* for several decades, appreciating only the beauty and wonder of the Sage's words, but without understanding what they were based on. Try as I would, I was unable to grasp the unifying principle. Occasionally, I appealed to those of the older generation who were steeped in the *I ching* in order to inquire what they had learned. They stressed the subtlety of its principles and the difficulty of glimpsing its secrets. Some are too metaphysical in their interpretation, and some are too numerological. Still others were too devoted to the art of divination.

All these aspects have been thoroughly discussed by the ancients, but I still was not satisfied. I turned then to the writings of the Confucian scholars, but they were only capable of superficially explaining the language of the text. As for the real intent of the words, this remained unclear. Why should the words of the sages be so difficult to understand? Was there no one who could provide the answer? This was most perplexing.

Forty-eight years ago, I had an opportunity to study the *I ching* with Su Hui-yüan. I heard him say that those who wrote on the *I ching* made many mistakes and that their study was without basis. Only Lai Chih-te's[1] commentary did he consider to transmit the true meaning of the images (*hsiang*). I studied this for several years and began to make some progress. In addition, I often discussed these matters with Ch'ien Chi-yüan's old classmate, Wang Chen. Wang was devoted to Ching Fang[2], and this was also very helpful to me.

Finally, last winter while visiting New York, I sustained a serious hip injury from a fall on an icy slope. Medication was applied over a very wide area, not only limiting movement, but even making reclining difficult. So sitting upright somewhat precariously, I read the *I ching* for distraction. After about ten days, suddenly all worries were stilled and my heart was like dead ashes. Quite unexpectedly, I experienced a realization. Was it possible that Confucius' diligent study was motivated by nothing but metaphysics, numerology, or divination? Did Confucius enjoy such abstract discussions of Heaven and earth? In his search for universal principles, did he have time for this? I perused the "Ten Wings"[3] seeking their central theme, and found that human conduct was primary. How could 2,000 years of Confucian scholars have overlooked this, to the point of blithely disregarding the main principle of the whole *I ching*?

I returned again to examine Lai's interpretation of the images, and for the first time realized that the commentaries of King Wen, the Duke of Chou, and Confucius were without a baseless word or false and empty phrase. I bitterly lamented that the words of the sages had been so twisted by misinterpretation. Through violation of reality and forced reasoning, the true spirit has been distorted and has fallen into the realm of the abstruse, further and further from the world of men.

Moreover, with Wang Pi's[4] sweeping away the images, the whole essence was destroyed. Therefore, Fan Ning of the Eastern Chin, who criticized him as equal to the villains Chieh and Chih, was not without justification. The Sung scholars followed his example, committing stupendous blunders and causing the *I ching* to languish in darkness for nineteen centuries. How grievous! The attacks of Ch'en [Tu-hsiu] and Ts'ai [Yüan-p'ei][5] lasted no more than days or weeks. Criticism of "Confucius and Sons"[6] was a calamity of only several decades. But the *I ching*'s misfortune has lasted more than 2,000 years, and it, indeed, may be considered the most unlucky. More recently, one hears of the Communist campaign to criticize Confucius, which is blasphemous and not worth mentioning. This ignorance of the *tao* of Confucius, like darkness covering the sun and moon, is a misfortune for all humanity.

In former days under the emperors, there were many obstacles and people feared censorship or punishment. But today in the midst of a cultural renaissance, I, despite great deficiencies, have written this *Complete I Ching*. My desire is to communicate Confucius' profound understanding of the *I ching* and humbly imitate the spirit of Kuo Wei[7], hoping that others will follow in the future. Truly, Confucius treated Yen Hui[8] as if he were his own nephew. Therefore, I humbly dare to set forth my learning undaunted by old age. Today, although I have reached the same age as the Master in his waning years, I make no excuses, but simply set down the main ideas, seeking to restore the honor of Confucius. As for the perfection of principles and greatness of literary style, this must wait for those of virtue and wisdom who come after me.

Notes:
1. 16th century Ming scholar.
2. Han dynasty scientist and *I ching* scholar.
3. Canonical commentaries to the *I ching*.
4. Wei dynasty *I ching* commentator.
5. Antifeudalists and advocates during the first half of this century of the New Culture Movement for national independence, individual freedom, and social justice.
6. Derogatory term coined by Hu Shih for Confucianism, taken as a synonym for the whole system of feudal morality.
7. Official who came out of seclusion during the Warring States period to serve King Chao of Yen and to aid in the destruction of Ch'i.
8. Confucius' most beloved disciple

XXII.
Selection on Medicine

From
Nü-k'e hsin-fa
(The essence of gynecology), Taipei: National Traditional Chinese Medicine Research Institute, 1961.

POSTERITY

The Way of posterity is based on the principles of natural transformation and does not depend on forced measures. Most of those who attempt to use force are disappointed. What can one expect from transgressing the laws of nature? According to my extensive experience in medical practice, if both man and woman are free of disease and abnormalities of disposition, there is no reason they should not be able to bear children. If there is a failure to conceive, the possibility of irregularities is equal for both sexes, and each should seek a good physician's care. It is possible to cure conditions, even of long standing.

Let me then briefly outline some of these conditions for the benefit of readers. Ninety percent of women's disorders have to do with menstrual problems or inflammation of the liver resulting in "drying up" of the blood. As for diseases of the reproductive organs, such as "spiral striations," it is rare to see one case in tens of thousands. These have already been discussed in detail above. Beyond these, illnesses such as uterine cancer or blockage of the Fallopian tubes must necessarily have their causes and if treated early are not difficult to cure. Male conditions include the following: nocturnal emissions, masturbation, venereal disease, premature ejaculation, impotence, thin semen, cold semen, diminutive sexual organ, erection without hardness, and hardness but inability to satisfy one's partner. All of these make conception difficult.

If both man and woman are free of the above disorders, but still have not conceived, they should observe the following:

1. One must nourish sexual energy (*ching*) and diminish desires. If sexual desire is excessive, then sexual energy will naturally be weak. How can one expect to conceive? Therefore the Classics say that the man should marry at thirty and the woman at twenty. This, too, is for the purpose of nourishing sexual energy and causing it to be abundant and strong. In this way one will receive great blessings with a single effort. To marry when the man is sixteen and woman fourteen is also possible, but one should be wary of marrying too early. The method of nourishing sexual energy is described in the medical classics. To summarize the important points: when a man is sixteen, after he has ejaculated once, it takes seven days for his *yang* to be renewed; at twenty four years of age it takes fourteen days; at thirty-two it takes twenty-one days. After forty, calculate one day of recovery for each year of age; thus at forty-one it takes forty-one days to renew one's *yang*, and the same would be true of forty-eight or nine, etc. After fifty, one should refrain from ejaculating altogether in order to protect one's life. Reckoning in this way, one can achieve great

longevity, even up to one hundred and twenty years. Therefore, one must be exceedingly careful. People today find this very difficult to practice, but nevertheless from the ages of thirty-two to forty-eight one should allow at least twenty days. More would be even better, for the method is simply to nourish the sexual energy and diminish desires.

2. Be moderate in exertion and slow to anger. Excessive physical activity is harmful to the kidneys [testes]. Excessive mental activity is harmful to the spleen. Frequent bouts of anger injure the liver. The liver stores the blood, the spleen controls the blood, and the kidneys are the "sea of blood." When these are injured, the blood becomes anemic. With anemia the sexual energy becomes weak and conception is difficult.

3. One should have intercourse at the proper time. Cats and dogs mate at definite times; how much more so is this appropriate for humans. The third to the fifth days after the woman's period is the proper time. The man's *yang* is born at the midnight hour and this is the most auspicious time. When there is no lightning, wind or rain, no vexation or anger, when one is not weary or drunk, and when the couple is full of passion for each other, this is the proper time.

The above points have been handed down from ancient times and need no further elaboration. Apart from this, modern Western theories or differences arising from place are beyond my purview. The ancients' writings on the art of the bedchamber are full of taboos which I do not subscribe to, thus for now I have been brief. Two prescriptions are presented below. Men and women can each take one or two doses. Both are beneficial to the body and facilitate conception.

For men:
- Dodder seeds (Cuscuta japonica), 8 ounces
- Parsley seeds (Cnidium monnieri), 5 ounces
- Psoralea corylifolia, 5 ounces
- Dried foxglove (Rehmannia glutinosa), 10 ounces
- Rubus tokkura, 5 ounces
- Plaintain seeds (Plantago major), 5 ounces
- Codonopsis cilosula, 8 ounces
- Fresh Dendrobium monile, 4 ounces
- White glutinous millet (Atractylis lancea), 2 ounces

Reduce and form into pills the size of dryandra seeds. Take six pills morning and evening.

For women:
- Dried foxglove, 12 ounces
- Fresh Dendrobium monile, 6 ounces
- Peisha ginseng, 5 ounces
- Fresh pear tree bark (Eucommia ulmoides), 5 ounces
- Asparagus lucidus and Lirione graminfolia, 2 ounces of each
- Dodder seeds, 6 ounces
- Juniper seed kernals (Biota orientalis), 2 ounces
- Loofah fibers, 1.5 ounces

Reduce and form into pills as above.

XXIII. Selections on the Arts

From
Man-jan san lun
(Three treatises
of Man-jan), Taipei:
Chung Hwa
Book Company, 1974.

SELECTIONS FROM
THREE TREATISES OF MAN-JAN

Author's Preface

These three short treatises on poetry, calligraphy, and painting represent sixty years of experience. I have no desire to be verbose and superficial. Poetry requires clarity and caution in speech and expressing one's nature in order to reveal one's will. Without this, it is no longer natural. Clever writers depart from the true and they hold nothing for us. We admire the great writers of ancient times for their flawless expression. Therefore it is said that blemishes in white jade still bear polishing, but blemishes in speech cannot be tolerated. It is also said that when words have left our mouth, galloping horses cannot retrieve them and thus in speaking one must be cautious. Secondly, if the superior man understands the larger picture, and his works are sound on the whole though defective in details, he will still be acclaimed as a famous writer. If there are many errors in one's words, even though one has produced some famous pieces or phrases which have been preserved by posterity, this is still shameful and not worthy of comparison with the great men of ancient times.

I was privileged to study with Master Ch'ien Shan whose ability to distinguish good and bad and to judge true and false I can never equal. However, this was not simply because he has older, well learned and had memorized a great deal by rote. If Li Po, Tu Fu, Han Yü, and Ou-yang Hsiu themselves were alive today, he would criticize their faults without embarrassment. Even if they were not willing to associate with us, I cannot believe they would not regard him with the highest respect. Most people commonly belittle the present and worship the past. They are nothing but pedants. Confucius did not have this attitude. Even his own disciple, Nan-kung K'uo, he praised as a man of the highest virtue. He also said, "Yung is worthy to serve as a ruler of men." When speaking of virute in men, there is no distinction of ancient and modern.

In discussing calligraphy I say only that horizontal and vertical strokes are like beams and posts; hide the head, protect the tail and seize the central peaks. Beyond this, left and right gaze at each other, and above and below follow each other, like older brother looking after younger brother and younger brother following older brother. To summarize: avoid violating principles and allow the *ch'i* to flow in a natural way. To proceed contrary to this and achieve lasting fame is nothing but luck. This sort does not win my admiration. I only understand love of the *tao*, which has nothing to do with individuals, how much less distinctions of ancient and modern.

My discussion of painting is based on calligraphy. I have no use for spiritless brushwork or tasteless ink. I have no use for those who over-emphasize form, nor those who ignore it. Rather we must honor spirit and make form subservient in order to approach true art. Form is to spirit as the common man is to the superior. Therefore it is said that when form is complete then spirit may manifest.

When it comes to brush and ink, they are precisely like the harmony of *ch'i* and blood. When the brush has too little ink, it becomes dry; when there is too little brush in the ink, it becomes blocked. Thus as *ch'i* is able to lead the blood, then we can see how the brush commands the ink. How can we allow the ink to overflow the brush? If the brush cannot control the ink and follow our will, then the results are inferior art. If the brush stands like a hog and the ink runs like a piglet and there is no understanding of the distinction between spirit and form, then one is simply an idiot. How can people such as these possibly discuss art?

In summary, when the spirit moves, the form comes alive; wherever the mind leads the brush follows. This, then, approaches true art. When my friend Meng Ku finished reading this work, he asked, "Is there one principle that unites poetry, calligraphy and painting?" I replied that there was. The ancients already united them. Calligraphy and painting originally issued from one source. Wang Wei's poetry contains paintings and his paintings contain poetry. Broad learning and the arts of poetry, calligraphy and painting flowed from the same hand and came together on one page, all united by inspiration. My three treatises are likewise united by one principle, and that is to express one's nature in order to reveal the will without departing from what is natural. My dear Meng Ku, do you have anything to add?

Spring, 1971, Man-jan

Preface to Book II, "On Calligraphy"

In the field of calligraphy, Li Ssu's introduction of the Lesser Seal style was an attempt to unify the writing system and eliminate unnecessary complexity in favor of convenience. This reform was not unreasonable. Prime Minister Hsiao Ho of the Former Han was well versed in the principles of calligraphy and used to discuss the art of the brush with Chang Liang, Ch'en Yin, and others. He said that the brush is the heart, the ink the hand, and calligraphy represents one's thought. By following this principle one naturally achieves marvelous results. Therefore Liu Kung-ch'üan said to the Emperor Mu Tsung, "The art of the brush is in the heart. If the heart is correct the brush is correct." Yen Lu-kung's [Chen-ch'ing] calligraphy was like he himself. His loyalty and righteousness were as clear as the sun and moon. From this we can see the contribution of calligraphy to the process of education. So I had much to gain from it. After we have said that calligraphy is like the man and that it reveals his heart, what else is there? If a person is unaware of this principle and attempts to discuss calligraphy, even if his style is as "lively as dragons leaping up to Heaven's gate and tigers crouching at the palace portal," nothing worthwhile can be learned from it.

Wang Hsi-chih's "Treatise on Calligraphy," which appears in Ch'en Ssu-chih's *Flowers from the Garden of Calligraphy (Shu-yüan ching-hua)*, begins with these words: "In calligraphy we do not value balance or stability." Is it coincidence that Han Yü referred to this as vulgar calligraphy which appeals through seductive pose? Later came the calligraphy of the likes of Mi Fei, Chao Meng-fu and Tung Ch'i-ch'ang and, though not without skill, they have nothing to offer from the point of view of their character and thought. Chang Hsü did not learn much, but he said simply that the horizontals should all be level, and one must not allow the verticals to be crooked. Yet this in itself was sufficient to make him a model for Yen

Chen-ch'ing. How can Chang Hsün's saying be correct: that by allowing the arm to move one cannot adhere to the true principles. In light of this, what are the implications for lack of balance and stability? Therefore in my essay on calligraphy, the horizontal and vertical strokes are considered to be the beams and posts that support a great building. The rest is just an extension of this idea.

When the heart is correct the brush is correct, and even if we simply mark a cross, our very deepest self is revealed. How can a man conceal himself? We can prove this by the way the ancients signed their names. They often used a cross. No one else could forge it precisely because it was a creation of their individual nature.

Before Ch'eng Miao and Li Ssu no one failed to use level horizontals and perpendicular verticals. From this we can see that the ancients did not dare to violate the carpenter's line. Yet some go so far as to say that when the strokes are balanced and proper, all calligraphy looks alike, that it appears like an abacus; when the dots do not change, they say it is like setting up a chessboard. They strenuously insist that it is wrong to use verticals and that there is no power in the straight. To use this as a basis for discussing calligraphy, together with their character and hearts, is far from the mark.

Great craftsmen teach according to the compass and the square and not according to clever tricks. Who dares to go against the chalk-line? Therefore, in discussing calligraphy, apart from the rules, I add only one word: *ch'i*. If, like Mencius, one can "excel at nourishing his great *ch'i*," then although they possess ten thousand techniques, they are all united by one. What need is there then for distinctions such as the "eight techniques" or the "nine techniques?" If one has *ch'i*, even if it appears like an abacus or chessboard, everything will function in a lively way; without *ch'i*, even if the horizontals are level and the verticals perpendicular, they will all be like flat corpses.

There are an infinite number of books which discuss all aspects of calligraphy and offer countless opinions. It is impossible to mention them all, and this, after all, has nothing to do with my purpose. I take my models from the Han and Wei dynasties and illustrate them with examples from the T'ang and Sung. Rather than ranging too broadly, I would prefer to receive one word that could serve as a guiding principle or one man who could serve as a teacher or a comrade. Let things be easy and thus easily understood, simple and thus simply fòllowed. That is all there is to it. Therefore Li Ssu's eliminating complexities in favor of what is better adapted was not a case of using his personal taste to cheapen the principles of calligraphy.

> 7th day, 1st lunar month, 1971,
> written in New York,
> Hsi-ch'ang Building, Man-jan

"The Past" from Book II, "On Calligraphy"

When I was six years old my mother began to teach me calligraphy. She had me suspend my elbow and hook my wrist. A glass of water was placed in the "tiger's mouth" of my hand and a tin coin balanced on top of the brush stem while I practiced the Han dynasty *Li* style according to the tradition handed down in my mother's family. By the age of ten I had strong suspicions and wondered why the ancients would resort to such methods. Later I learned that it was not an ancient method, but merely one advocated by Pao Shih-ch'en of the Ch'ing. I surmised that he basically had two ideas in mind: first, to prevent the fingers from shaking and the wrist from trembling, and second, to gradually strengthen the power of the wrist. When I explained this reasoning to my mother she agreed with me, and so we abandoned this technique. We then adopted the "Stirrup Method" of holding the brush transmitted by Lady Wei which emphasized moving the elbow but not the wrist and focusing one's entire spirit in order to develop the power of the brush.

One day in the marketplace I saw a collotype edition of Wang Hsi-chih's "Broken Tablet" (*Pan-chieh pei*). I was overjoyed and purchased it as if obtaining the most precious treasure. I felt that nothing had ever been produced to equal it. Not long after that, I obtained a fine edition of Ming rubbings and practiced from these two for twelve years without interruption. I was later admonished by Lo Fu-k'an that it was difficult for one to develop while imitating Wang Hsi-chih, and he advised me to study instead Li Pei-hai's "Lu-shan Temple Tablet." In less than half a year I became well known as a calligrapher, but I was dissatisfied with it being too easy and so abandoned it and once again returned to my study of the Seal and Clerical styles. One day Cheng Su-k'an saw me copying from the "Stone Gate Ode" (*Shih-men sung*) and approvingly said that I must go immediately to Shanghai and sell my works. He predicted that within three years if he came to visit me, I would have no time to receive him and would be a very rich man.

Later I thought about this and concluded that my calligraphy certainly had a commercial look and I ceased copying that style. I then started once again studying the calligraphy from the Three Dynasties [Hsia, Shang, and Chou] all the way up to the T'ang, over and over for ten years, yet I could not figure out how to escape Wang Hsi-chih's influence and stood bewildered at a crossroads. At the age of 30, I thereupon determined to write the characters with steadiness and not to think of anything else.

One day after relocating in Taiwan, Chu Ting came to visit me and highly praised my calligraphy. I answered, "I do not have your balance and really cannot compare with your weight." I continued saying, "I looked for one word for twenty years and could not find it."

Ting was very surprised and asked, "What character did you study?"

I then wrote the character *wen* (steady). Ting struck the table with his hand and exclaimed, "You labored twenty years for just this one word?"

I turned the question around and asked him, "My friend, why is your calligraphy so well balanced?"

He answered, "One day I asked the Buddhist monk Hung-i to instruct me in calligraphy." He replied, "Do you really want to learn calligraphy?"

"I said, "Yes, I sincerely do."

He said, "If you can first devote three years to practicing the character *yi* (— ,one) with balance, then I will agree to teach you."

I said, "Really?"

He said, "Yes."

Ting practiced for three years, and when he could write the character *yi* with balance, he went to Hung-yi.

Hung-yi said, "This is good. You have accomplished the goal."

Ting then practiced writing a single vertical stroke so that it was perfectly perpendicular. Just this and nothing more. I applauded Ting and laughed out loud. Although I have pursued the quality of steadiness for forty years, yet it is still often not easy to achieve balance and verticality. That for forty or fifty years I have fallen under Wang Hsi-chih's influence and have not been able to extricate myself from this trap, can truly be called a chronic habit. Now as I speak of the past I cannot keep from sighing and so take this opportunity to record the error of my ways.

"A New Interpretation of the 'Stirrup Method' of Holding the Brush" from Book II, "On Calligraphy"

According to tradition, the "Stirrup Method" of holding the brush was transmitted by Lady Wei to Wang Hsi-chih, but why do neither of them mention this in their essays on calligraphy or in other writings? Moreover, it is not likely that Wei was well versed in horsemanship, so how is it she used the manner of placing the foot in the stirrup as a comparison for holding the brush? I am very skeptical. Furthermore, the explanations of the function of the "Stirrup Method" by Huai Su, Lin Yün, and others of the T'ang period, were not completely to the point, but the rest can be surmised.

I know that beginning with Hsiao Ho of the Han many methods for achieving excellence in calligraphy have been handed down. How then can it be that there are no mnemonic verses for holding the brush? It is because they relied on oral instruction for transmission from generation to generation. To insist on referring to this as "Lady Wei's Stirrup Method" is not as appropriate as simply saying that it was transmitted by Chung Yüan-ch'ang. As far as whom Chung received it from, this need not be fully ascertained, nor is there any point to it.

Han Fang-ming of the T'ang, in teaching the essentials of the brush, said that holding the brush is the secret of wonderful calligraphy. Ch'en Ssu of the Sung said that when beginning to study calligraphy the most important concern is holding the brush. I use Hsiao Ho and Ts'ai Yung's method of holding the brush and believe we are not too far from each other. In fact, in the "The Eight Techniques of the Character *Yung*," the two strokes, bridle [horizontal] and whip [rising diagonal] both have to do with horsemanship and seem to imply some relationship to this. Lin Yün of the T'ang said that the meaning of "stirrup" is that when holding the brush, the "tiger's mouth" is empty and round like a stirrup. When the foot is placed in the stirrup, it should not be inserted deeply, so as to facilitate ease of movement. Huai Su said that when two men ride, their stirrups must not interfere with each other. Neither of these are satisfactory explanations. I simply explain it by saying that the length of the stirrup hanging from the saddle should be equal to the length of the rider's leg, and that when the pen is held in the hand the energy should issue from the shoulder. Thus this is referred to as "hanging elbows." The pen is held by the fingers, thus the palm is empty and the fingers full, just like the foot in the stirrup which according to the art of horsemanship must not be inserted too deeply. If a person not skilled in horsemanship inserts the foot too deeply into the stirrup and allows it hang in the stirrup, then it simply hangs there as if dead and completely loses its ability to function. If they are not careful and the horse falls, then they are in serious danger. Therefore using the placement of the foot in the stirrup as a metaphor for holding the brush is profound and eloquent and not just a vague generalization. When moving the brush with the fingers, make the palm empty like a stirrup.

Ch'ien Jo-shui of the Sung said that among the great calligraphers of old few truly possessed the art of the brush. Hsi Sheng of the T'ang possessed the art and summarized it in five words: *yen* (push), *ya* (press), *kou* (hook), *chü* (resist), *ko* (attack). When holding the brush the hand forms two hooks; then the strokes will have power and be truly marvelous. This is called the "Stirrup Method." Ch'en Yi-ts'eng of the Yüan in his *Secrets of the Han-lin (Han-lin yao-chüeh)* explained the principles of calligraphy in these words, "The method of holding the brush consists of eight finger techniques: one is *yen* (push), wherein the bottom side of the last digit of the thumb applies strength, straightening as if raising a thousand weight. Two is *na* (press), or what Li Yü calls *ya* (press), wherein the index finger makes contact with the brush at the side of the middle joint. Thus the two top fingers [thumb and index] are the controlling force. In three, *kou* (hook), the middle finger makes contact at the tip of the finger "hooking" the brush and directing it downward. In four, *chieh* (lift), the outer surface of the fourth finger makes contact with the brush, lifting it in an upward direction. In five, *ti* (resist), the fourth finger seeks to lift the brush but the middle finger "resists", holding it steady. In six, *chü* (oppose), the middle finger hooks the brush while the ring finger opposes it, holding it in place. The three top fingers control the rotation. In seven, *tao* (lead), the little finger "leads" the fourth finger to the right. In eight, *sung* (send), the little finger "sends" the fourth finger to the left. Thus the bottom finger controls the back and forth movement."

The preceding eight techniques are called the "Stirrup Method." I do not know what this passage is based on, but it is somewhat more detailed than Ch'ien Jo-shui's essay. However, it is confused and complicated and lacking in reason. Allow me to rectify this. The eight word transmission of the "Stirrup Method" is the application of the six combined energies of the four cardinal directions together with above and below. One is *yen* (push), wherein the strength of the thumb is great and it pushes straight ahead and level. In two, *ya* (press), the index finger is no match in strength for the thumb and thus sits in an elevated position somewhat bent and applies strength pressing inwards, thereby balancing the strength and advantage of the thumb. In this way, the two directions, front and rear, are maintained in equilibrium. In three, *kou* (hook), the middle finger is the longest and can embrace the brush from the right, forming a hook. These are the three fingers occupying the uppermost position. They can also be called the "Heavenly Trinity." There are three partners in this trinity and each contributes its strength to one direction. In four, *chü* (oppose), the ring finger applies strength in mutual opposition, outwards and towards the left. However, it cannot equal the hooking strength of the middle finger and therefore in five, *ti* (resist), the little finger sticks to the back of the ring finger helping to withstand the hooking power of the middle finger. Thus the power of the left and right are in equilibrium. In this way, the power of the four directions—front, back, left, and right—is complete. However, the power of the Heavenly Trinity above, with three fingers weighing down, is excessively strong. How can it be balanced? Therefore, the combined strength of the ring and little fingers is called the "Earthly Pair." The two combine together, and because they occupy the lower position, we call them earth. Even though the power of the Heavenly Trinity is great, the forces are divided into three areas. Even though the power of the Earthly Pair is somewhat weak, nevertheless, the strength is combined and together controls one direction alone, so that the whole is maintained in balance. Therefore six, *chieh* (lift), means to raise something up in order to match the power of the downward pressure and thus maintain the balance of power above and below. This, then, is the power balance of the six directions. In seven, *tao* (lead), because of the united strength of the five fingers, the little finger is not able to play an independent role, therefore we speak of "leading." Leading means to guide. The ring finger is guided towards the right. This is the hidden power of the rotation of earth (*k'un*). Eight is *sung* (send), meaning that since the earth rotates, Heaven is always in revolution. Therefore the ring finger is sent towards the left, and thus there is opening and closing. In this way, the earth rotates and Heaven revolves. This is my rectification of the old theory. As to whether it is appropriate or not, we must await the judgment of future men of ability.

"Explaining Power" from Book II, "On Calligraphy"

Lin Yün of the T'ang, in creating the "Stirrup Method," said that it was transmitted by An Ch'i who was a second generation disciple of Lu Chao. After more than a year, old Lu suddenly said to him, "You have been studying my style of calligraphy, but seek only its power. Do you not know that brush power is not found in power itself? When we use power the brush dies. If instead, we empty the palm and substantiate the fingers and do not let the fingers penetrate the palm, then where is any obstacle east or west, up or down?" Lu Chao's statement that if strength is used, the brush is dead is subtle indeed! Unfortunately, this has nothing to do with emptying the palm and substantiating the fingers and falls short of expressing the correct idea. When the palm is empty and the fingers full, is it not still possible to use strength? Furthermore, if we do use strength, is not the brush dead? Nevertheless, Chao's desire to analyze power is still very wonderful.

Men like Chung and Chang did not have completely satisfactory explanations of power. From ancient times it has been handed down that in grasping the shaft of the brush one should use strength, so that if someone approached us from behind and attempted to snatch the brush from our hand, they could not succeed. When I was young I was taught by my mother who gradually added tin coins to the top of my brush in order to increase the strength of my fingers. Later in life, when forced to flee to Chungking, I often had discussions with Shen Yin-mo, Wang Tung, and Ch'en Fang. One day we touched on the subject of handling the brush, and Yin-mo said that in holding the brush one should not use strength. I was puzzled and could not understand, so I asked about it. He said that the fingers and brush should be completely natural, and it is just that one must not use dead strength.

At that time, I was not able to grasp the meaning of this theory. Now let us explain it a bit further. If you give the shaft of a brush to an infant, you will not be able to take it back. This is what Lao Tzu meant by saying that when the sinews are soft, the grip is firm, for all is lively power. If one intuitively grasps this saying, then Lu Chao's meaning will be realized.

To put an end to all of these differences over the correct method of holding the brush, I will speak here very frankly. Ts'ai Yung's "Nine Powers" says that "applying the brush with strength makes for beauty of flesh and skin," and in explaining the "Eight Techniques" it is also said that "strength is the essence." However, this falls short of revealing the secret. With the discovery of Wei Yen's tomb, Chung Yu obtained Ts'ai Yung's "Treatise on Brush Power" and for the first time understood that "those with much strength and full sinews are divine, while those without strength or sinews are defective." These words revealed the secret, but Chung Yu was not able to interpret its hidden essence. Thus I have never heard of a true transmission of this.

What is meant by "much strength" is not really strength, but energy (*chin*). My fellow student Ch'en Hsiao-lien (Wei-ming) studied T'ai chi ch'üan for several decades, but when it came to the difference between strength and energy, he was not able to get to the bottom of it. Not long after that I received the secret teaching of Master Tsuo Lai-p'eng of Shansi which stated that strength issues from the bones, but energy issues from the sinews. In a burst of clarity I was enlightened. Forty years ago I wrote these words in my *Master Cheng's Thirteen Chapters on Tai-chi ch'üan* in order to share them with fellow students and spread the transmission.

What Ts'ai Yung meant by "great strength and full sinews" is precisely that power which issues from the sinews is energy (*chin*). Moreover, his saying "conceal the head, round the brush, focus on the paper and cause the heart of the brush to move always within the dots and strokes," together with the rules for horizontals, downward diagonals, verticals, and upward diagonals all indicate where energy is produced. This is in the same vein as my contention that a powerful brush comes from the energy of the sinews: Lao Tzu's secret lies therein. Was Chung Yu able to understand the reason for this? I am afraid he did not.

I am now seventy years old and am not willing to take this secret to the grave. I am also not willing like Chung Yu and Wang Hsi-chih to selfishly transmit it only to my sons. My only hope is that students will gain a deep appreciation of it.

1971

"Establishing the Foundation" from Book II, "On Calligraphy"

What do we mean by establishing the foundation? The purpose of discussing the "Stirrup Method" of holding the brush, learning the brush strokes based on character *yung* 永 , and the "Nine Techniques," together with our interpretation of power and the use of ink, all has to do with establishing the foundation. But these still only describe the curriculum of study for establishing the foundation and not the root of it. The root of establishing the foundation is *ch'i*.

The strength which issues from the bones cannot be said to be without *ch'i*, and the energy (*chin*) which issues from the sinews is nothing other than *ch'i*. What further distinctions can there be of *ch'i*? The strength which issues from the bones is simply the spirited courage of the blood's *ch'i*. The *ch'i* of the blood begins in the gall bladder and issues from the liver. The energy that issues from the sinews is the *ch'i* of sexual energy (*ching*), that is, primordial *ch'i* which originated in the kidneys [testes]. The kidneys are life, the root. This is the root of establishing the foundation.

What do we mean by establishing the foundation? It is like constructing a building. The foundation is the first task. Its function is strength and stability. How does a calligrapher lay a foundation? We say that it is simply sinking the *ch'i* to the *tan-t'ien* and touching the earth with the sole of the foot. The *ch'i* should be moved to the shoulders, the elbows, the wrists, the fingers, and finally to the tip of the brush. This is the essence of it. This is what is meant by a discipline with root. Without it, the brush just runs on and on wildly. But if one proceeds with root, then like pines, bamboo, cane, and vines that grow freely in accordance with their natures, there is never the least gracelessness in its appearance. Because it is natural there is no hint of affectation. If affectation enters into artistic work, although one is received at court and showered with honors, men of true cultivation will not be impressed. Therefore I believe that those who are rooted in *ch'i*, though they have mastered the "Eight Techniques" or the "Nine Techniques," their execution will be based on the one.

What then is meant by saying that many styles enter into one character? If one writes a whole page of characters, each character must represent a different idea and none can be the same. This is so obvious only young children need to be told. But then there are conscientious students who show achievement in two months, and those who are naturally gifted and grasp the root within a hundred days. This theory of calligraphy was considered a family treasure or family jewel and kept secret. This was very confusing to me. Chung Yu practiced ceaselessly for ten or thirty years, but only after obtaining Ts'ai Yung's "Treatise on Calligraphy" did he understand that "much strength and full sinews are divine, whereas no strength and no sinews are defects." How easy it is to talk of seeing achievement and grasping the root in two months or a hundred days. The twelve chapters of the "Treatise on Calligraphy" go on and on plagirizing from other writers and never explain "much strength and full sinews." If this is what is considered a transmission of secret family treasures and jewels, in reality, it is merely a display of great waves and soaring atmosphere, capable only of deluding people.

What I mean by establishing a foundation is not as easy as this. It is not limited to a period of ten or thirty years, or even a lifetime. It must be with us whether sleeping or eating. Our task must be to correct faults and seek balance and stability without ambition for profit or hollow fame. Instead we must "excel at nourishing our great *ch'i*," directing it from the *tan-t'ien* to the waist, the backbone, the shoulders, the elbows, the wrists, the fingers and finally reaching the tip of the brush. This is like saying, "wherever the sword goes the shoes go" or "wherever the mind goes the *ch'i* has already arrived." We might also say that the mind precedes the brush and moves together with the *ch'i*. The theory of establishing the foundation is just this.

1971

"Eight Introductory Essays" from Book III, "On Painting"

1. Ability.

Ability is competence. For beginners, competence means first acquiring accuracy. First seek manual accuracy. A scene enters the eye and emerges from the hand. There should not be the slightest error in reproducing what strikes the eye. This is manual accuracy. Next seek visual accuracy. When a scene strikes the eye one can distinguish the beautiful and the grotesque, the gross and the fine, without leaving out a detail. When the observations of the eye can respond to the mind, this is visual accuracy. When the eye is already trained to observe carefully, but it seems for the moment that there is nothing to see, then the problem is a lack of refinement in the mind and not in the eye. If in observing things, one fails to thoroughly grasp the outline and the details, then the fault lies in a lack of visual accuracy and inability to coordinate with the mind. Thus, the accuracy of the hand is determined by the mind, and if the mind functions correctly, then we can be sure that the function of the eye is in harmony with the mind. If something arises in the mind, there can be a response in the hand and the eye will also be aware of it. These are the "Three Unities." If something arises in the mind and the hand cannot respond, then the eye too will not be able to follow it. Thus the fault is not in the eye, but in the lack of accuracy of the hand. Therefore, beginners must first seek the accuracy of the hand, and when the hand is accurate, then more than half the battle will be won.

2. Power.

Power refers to the power of the brush. Although the hand may be accurate, it does not necessarily have power. In seeking to achieve accuracy, the brush is moved slowly and the power is weak, for it is difficult to realize accuracy when moving quickly. Power can only come after achieving accuracy of the hand and it should be cultivated gradually. At the highest level of accomplishment, the faster the brush moves, the more power manifests. This is simple.

Among those displaying much power there is "spear and club *ch'i*" and "grass and earth *ch'i*," but these are not true power, for they are merely external. When expressed externally, power is superficial, but power that is full within, reaching all the way to the root, appears to be without power. When it is thoroughly mastered one feels that the movement of power knows no impediment. This is called intrinsic energy (*chin*). Intrinsic energy is externally soft but hard within and flexible. This is true power. With true power one is lively, but without it, stiff. Now where does true power come from? Ch'an Master Chih Kui tells us to rotate the right shoulder and relax the left foot in order to mobilize the power of the waist. Li Pei-hai says that when applying the brush, the two feet press as if seeking to break the floor boards. This refers to our rooting power which arises from the feet. Yen Lu-kung said that power arises from the toes of the feet. This is *ch'i* whose power rises up from the root. Thus is revealed what others before had not yet revealed. Teachings like "the stain left by a roof leak," "bending hairpins," "printing with seal ink," and "drawing in the sand with an awl" are all extensions of this idea. What I have learned is to sit erect or to stand straight with the sole of the left foot sticking to the floor. One should sink the *ch'i* and then begin to work. At the outset of learning to manipulate the brush one should concentrate on simplicity. Simplicity makes it easy to be accurate. After achieving accuracy, practice faithfully and power will appear. When power is sufficient and the will undivided, one gradually reaches a spiritual state and it is then not difficult to achieve transcendence.

3. Learning.

The wise men of former times said that if we examine the value of traveling ten thousand miles or reading ten thousand books, it is nothing other than learning. Now, a journey of ten thousand miles is very long and a study of ten thousand books is comprehensive indeed, but if one has gained intellectually and can make practical use of it, then it is surely valuable. However, today one can travel ten thousand miles in a single day and possess broad learning in spite of evil intentions. Does this deserve to be considered true devotion to learning and practical application? Therefore what I mean by the difference between the scholar's painting and the painter's painting is simply the difference between learning or the lack of it, self-cultivation or the lack of it. To peruse ten thousand books and know the words and deeds of the past in order to accumulate virtue, to travel ten thousand miles and experience the many mountains, rivers and forests as well as the ways and customs of the people in order to broaden one's knowledge, to enrich this with letters and express it in calligraphy and painting makes one's thought realm profound and one's bosom capacious and gives one the wherewithal to rise above the common. This then is learning which is well-rounded and expresses itself in practical use. Kuan Chung, Chu Ko-liang, Kuan Ning, T'ao Ch'ien, Yüeh Fei, Wen T'ien-hsiang and Shih K'o-fa were all scholars, and although their fields of application were all different, their devotion to learning was the same. Today to approach calligraphy and painting from a background in learning is to reveal one's righteousness and liberality, one's lofty and faithful spirit, and to give it beautiful form with paper and ink. It can lead the people in virtuous ways, create great imperishable works, and be nearly the equal of the ancients. Is it merely a pleasant pastime, self-expression, or an exercise in non-action?

4. Consciousness.

People dislike lofty vision but poor technique. In reality, without lofty vision there is no guarantee of superior technique. Instead we should say that only if the vision is lofty can technique be superior. If the vision is lofty and the technique not equal to it, this can be remedied with time, Lofty vision is consciousness. Consciousness precedes everything. Men of foresight are invariably so because of consciousness. We do not know where consciousness comes from. Is it not truth? Truth is of Heaven and consciousness of man. The unity of Heaven and man produces consciousness. The opposite of this is man-made artifice. Wearing out one's mind and becoming duller every day simply lowers one's consciousness to the point that it becomes irremediable. If beginning students are not sincere in their pursuit of truth and if their brush strokes are not clearly distinguished and the models not faithfully followed, how can one expect to reach the level of complete ease and facility? This is why truth produces clarity. *Ch'i* is nothing other than clarity, and this is the origin of consciousness. Dots and strokes are the foundation of calligraphy and painting. Without truth and consciousness, learning and experience, one can accomplish nothing. This, then, is what makes consciousness, *consciousness.* What is called "thought realm" is produced by none other than consciousness. But if one wants to attain mental superiority, no amount of broad learning and careful inquiry will suffice without truth and single-mindedness.

5. Realizing faults.

Faults mean that there are blocks which we are not aware of and which impede us. What are faults? They include being mired in tradition, following the latest trends, clinging to a master's teachings, creating foolish novelties, having the ambition to set up one's own school, emphasizing eclecticism, and being blinded by ink or corrupted by color. With these various conditions, the faults are easily understood and easily apprehended. If one can become aware of and strive to eliminate them, it should not be difficult. Those faults which are not easily recognized and are difficult to eliminate are subtle and miniscule; without great effort to uncover them they are impossible to recognize, and without hard work and painful correction are impossible to uproot. In general, after thorough investigation, they include clumsiness of form and loss of spirit, clumsy use of color and lack of taste, clumsy brushwork and starved *ch'i*, clumsy *ch'i* and failure of the whole work, weakness without suppleness, crudeness without strength, thickness without depth, disorganization without expansiveness, palor without elegance, or antique appearance but common taste. These can all be detected, realized, and with effort eliminated. However, when it comes to a slanted brush but flat ink, overflowing ink and soaked brush, a light brush and flowing ink, stiff ink and a flat brush, a delicate brush and weak ink, diffuse ink and a broad brush, a broken brush and scattered ink, or dense ink and a constrained brush, the error is in the teaching or not having a teacher. Once they have become habitual, even if one is able to identify them, it is still not easy to correct. Therefore, it is easiest to eliminate faults at the beginning stages. Once faults have taken hold, they cannot be corrected without great determination.

How can we be without faults? Let me expand on this a bit. Faults of brush and ink are like sickness in the internal organs. They are not easily cured. The rest are merely superficial and easily cured once we become aware of them. If we can avoid faults, then what sickness is there to speak of?

Now if we want to spread the brush, we must quickly withdraw it, for if the ink splashes it is a great pity. If we desire to withdraw the brush and penetrate the paper, then the ink becomes as fine as cast iron. If the brush gallops with perfect ease, then the ink flies in all directions like unfolding patterned silk. If we "hide the brush tip" like wood-boring insects, then the ink drips down in a concentrated flow. When the brush comes down like falling rain, the ink is like ranks of soldiers. If the brush now withdraws and then advances, and the ink swallows and spits, then the brush is like rising mist and the ink is like birds spreading their wings. Thus by analogy and indirection one cannot only become aware of faults, but also reach the level of perfect ease. If students do not begin with this in mind, then faults will appear in numbers too great for me to describe.

6. Understanding change.

There are three conditions under which change should not take place and three when it should. Before one has achieved a certain level of ability one cannot change. Before one's knowledge is sufficient one cannot change. Before one's level of skill has developed one cannot change. These are the three conditions under which change should not take place. If one has already thoroughly mastered a teacher's method, one must change. If one follows the ancients and has thoroughly grasped their meaning, one must change. If a teacher has exhausted his creativity, one must change. These are the three conditions under which one cannot but change. Those of great talent undergo great changes, while those of small talent undergo small changes. Among those who are not able to change, either their talent or learning is not sufficient. I have never known anyone with talent who did not change. I have never known those to succeed who desire to change but are not ready. The molted shells of cicada represent change. The chrysalis of the silk worm that becomes a moth also represents change. Is it possible for them to change before the proper time? Therefore, without talent and before the proper time, it is foolish to forcibly seek change.

If we want to thoroughly understand the nature of change, we may look to calligraphy and painting. Chung Yu's calligraphy is dense and weighty and the feeling emerges; it is classic and simple and the form appears. Wang Hsi-chih's calligraphy is completely different. Its modesty comes from feeling and its looseness manifests in the form. This is his great transformation. Li Ssu-hsün and Mi Yüan-chang's paintings are each different in respect to feeling and form, and their sons were worthy successors. Although all of them maintained the family tradition, there still was a desire for change. None of them were as talented as their fathers, and therefore the changes were minor.

From the point of view of the design, the medium and the scene each mountain, river, flower and tree, each brush stroke and element manifests its transformations. When a mountain is sheer and craggy but without mist, clouds, and trees to shroud it, then it will suffer from rarification of *ch'i*. For an expanse of water to be without declevities or reeds to break it up, it will suffer from stiffness. To scatter flowers without rocks to pin them down, or to have dense trees without bamboo to break them up, from a single brush stroke to a whole scene, our greatest fear should be stiffness and mere copying. All of this illustrates the difference between understanding change and not understanding change. The distance or depth of brush and ink, the realm of opacity and transparency, *yin* and *yang*, opening and closing, and primary and subordinate elements invariably change in accordance with the artistic conception.

My discussion of change is like the myriad fruits, grasses, and trees. Their leaves are in some cases giant and some very fine, but their color is always green. They receive the *ch'i* of Heaven and earth and the colors black [Heaven] and yellow [earth] and transform as they grow and live. If one speaks of change that deviates from nature, then I dare not have knowledge of this. In the transformations of leopards and tigers each simply fulfills its kind.

7. Creation.

How can creativity be an easy subject to discuss? Wang Wang-ch'uan used pale washes to execute landscapes and Hsü Ch'ung-ssu used "bonelessness" to portray flowers and birds, yet both established the Southern School of painting and created a unique style. Mi Yüan-chang painted rainy scenes with large misty patches and Chao Tzu-ku used sketching technique to portray the narcissus. They also created their own styles, though rarely seen. This is truly what is meant by the saying, "wherever water flows a stream will naturally form." The twists and turns of mountain ranges follow the laws of nature and cannot be forced. The present preoccupation with creativity and creating what has never before been seen, like Ts'ang Chieh's invention of writing or Ta Nao's inventing the "Heavenly branches and earthly stems" is truly not an easy matter. Thus from the bosom of nature and with the application of craftsmanship and the work of natural transformation, then and only then is success possible. It has ever been thus from ancient times.

How many men do we know of over the last few thousand years who have reached this level? It is an accident when one man receives the gift, but not an accident for he who seeks it. Some study for five years, ten years, or several decades, but whether they will succeed or not cannot be predicted. There may be a hundred men, a thousand or ten thousand, but no one can say who will succeed. If they do succeed it is undoubtedly because their natural talent and capacity for study are superior to others. If students are able to forsake fame and fortune, avoid impatience and haste, give up superstition and eccentricity, refrain from displaying their cleverness and love of learning, and find a superior teacher and study diligently, they can then transform their dispositions, and even the dull will become brilliant and the handicapped reach the goal. When their art is mature, how can they not desire to create? The mind follows whatever the eye makes contact with, and the hand responds to whatever the mind receives. Thus gaining advantage from all sides and maintaining happiness and contentment, there is creativity in all we do, and success follows at every turn.

8. Reckoning Mastery.

What do we mean by mastery in learning? It is like shipping goods for trade. While the goods are still en route they cannot yet be reckoned. Some study Chung in the morning and Wang in the evening, and spend their whole lives in confusion without being faithful to one. How can we consider this true learning? There are some who have studied barely a few years and are already able to maintain the basic principles. People say that so-and-so is a disciple of Chung and refer to the style of his school as Chung, calling him a noted artist. Others study Wang and are simply placed in the Wang camp. People say that so-and-so has studied Wang and perfected this style. Some study the calligraphy of both Chung and Wang, and grasping the spirit of each, develop a style of their own. This is called establishing one's own school. However, those who establish their own schools recognize only themselves. But what I mean by mastery is a step beyond recognizing ourselves. Mastery means achieving one's own mastery, not the mastery of Chung or Wang.

What can we say to those who wish to pursue this? We can say that it is like drinking water. It is not enough to know if its nature is mild or hot or cold. It is not enough to distinguish whether its taste is salty or bland or sweet. It is not enough to investigate its consistency or its weight. It is not enough to ascertain the sallowness or whiteness of its color or its darkness or brightness. It is not even enough to seek to know its clarity or impurity or the relative degree of each. It is not even enough to seek to know the dryness, moistness, or excessive dampness of what one has gained, but by finally getting to the origin of the source and the direction of the flow, one can begin to grasp the entire essence. This then can be called mastery.

Is it any different with the arts? If one desires to get to the heart of the matter, then how should one practice to achieve mastery? We say, grasp the main ideas, develop your power, be single-minded in your ambition, keep cutting and never give up, and have no regrets. Afterwards, seek only forward progress and in this way one may become a great master. Can we call this only mastery?

Man-jan, early 1952, Taiwan

displaying their cleverness and love of learning, and find a superior teacher and study diligently, they can then transform their dispositions, and even the dull will become brilliant and the handicapped reach the goal. When their art is mature, how can they not desire to create? The mind follows whatever the eye makes contact with, and the hand responds to whatever the mind receives. Thus gaining advantage from all sides and maintaining happiness and contentment, there is creativity in all we do, and success follows at every turn.

8. Reckoning Mastery.

What do we mean by mastery in learning? It is like shipping goods for trade. While the goods are still en route they cannot yet be reckoned. Some study Chung in the morning and Wang in the evening, and spend their whole lives in confusion without being faithful to one. How can we consider this true learning? There are some who have studied barely a few years and are already able to maintain the basic principles. People say that so-and-so is a disciple of Chung and refer to the style of his school as Chung, calling him a noted artist. Others study Wang and are simply placed in the Wang camp. People say that so-and-so has studied Wang and perfected this style. Some study the calligraphy of both Chung and Wang, and grasping the spirit of each, develop a style of their own. This is called establishing one's own school. However, those who establish their own schools recognize only themselves. But what I mean by mastery is a step beyond recognizing ourselves. Mastery means achieving one's own mastery, not the mastery of Chung or Wang.

What can we say to those who wish to pursue this? We can say that it is like drinking water. It is not enough to know if its nature is mild or hot or cold. It is not enough to distinguish whether its taste is salty or bland or sweet. It is not enough to investigate its consistency or its weight. It is not enough to ascertain the sallowness or whiteness of its color or its darkness or brightness. It is not even enough to seek to know its clarity or impurity or the relative degree of each. It is not even enough to seek to know the dryness, moistness, or excessive dampness of what one has gained, but by finally getting to the origin of the source and the direction of the flow, one can begin to grasp the entire essence. This then can be called mastery.

Is it any different with the arts? If one desires to get to the heart of the matter, then how should one practice to achieve mastery? We say, grasp the main ideas, develop your power, be single-minded in your ambition, keep cutting and never give up, and have no regrets. Afterwards, seek only forward progress and in this way one may become a great master. Can we call this only mastery?

Man-jan, early 1952, Taiwan